THE ROSWELL UFO CONSPIRACY

EXPOSING A SHOCKING
AND SINISTER SECRET

Published by Lisa Hagan Books 2017

www.lisahaganbooks.com

Powered by

SHADOW
TEAMS

ISBN: 9781945962042

Cover art work photography courtesy of CJA Imaging

Cover design and interior layout by Simon Hartshorne

+ + + NICK REDFERN + + +

THE ROSWELL UFO CONSPIRACY

EXPOSING A SHOCKING AND SINISTER SECRET

Also with Lisa Hagan Books:

Men in Black: Personal Stories & Eerie Experiences
Women in Black: The Creepy Companions of the Mysterious M.I.B.
365 Days of UFOs: A Year of Alien Encounters

For all titles by Nick Redfern, see his page on
Amazon.com or http://nickredfernfortean.blogspot.com

CONTENTS

INTRODUCTION

WHEN it comes to the issue of what really happened on what was once known as the Foster Ranch, Lincoln County, New Mexico in early July 1947, there are things we know, things we suspect, and things we will probably never know. But, that *something* happened – something which caused the U.S. Air Force to offer multiple explanations for the event – is not a matter of any doubt at all. It was an incident that clearly concerned elements of not just the military, but the government, too, and to a highly significant degree. Eye-witnesses – both military and civilian – were warned not to talk about what they had seen and/or heard. More than a few of those warnings crossed the line and can only accurately be described as death threats. People were plunged into states of fear. Lives were changed forever; even scarred. Some lives may have ended; as in terminated.

It was on July 8, 1947 that the strange event surfaced publicly. Associated Press (among many other news outlets) reported on the startling, then-breaking news:

> "The many rumors regarding the flying disc became a reality yesterday when the intelligence office of the 509th Bomb Group of the Eighth Air Force, Roswell Army Air Field, was fortunate enough to gain possession of a disc through the cooperation of one of the local ranchers and the sheriff's office of Chavez County.
>
> "The flying object landed on a ranch near Roswell sometime last week. Not having phone facilities,

> the rancher stored the disc until such time as he was able to contact the sheriff's office, who in turn notified Major Jesse A. Marcel of the 509th Bomb Group Intelligence Office.
>
> "Action was immediately taken and the disc was picked up at the rancher's home. It was inspected at the Roswell Army Air Field and subsequently loaned by Major Marcel to higher headquarters."

The story was quickly picked up not just across the United States, but across the planet too. In barely no time at all, however, the flying disc angle was blown out of the sky: the whole thing was nothing but a huge, embarrassing mistake. The materials found on the massive ranch – by rancher William Ware "Mack" Brazel – were not the remains of a disc after all. What had really been found, and subsequently collected and brought to the Roswell Army Air Field, was weather-balloon debris. Or, so the military was careful to assure everyone.

With Brazel at the time of the discovery – which had actually occurred days earlier – was a young boy named Dee Proctor. He would go on to be one of the most important people in the Roswell story. We also know for sure that three, key military men, all of whom were destined to become part and parcel of the Roswell affair, were also present at the ranch – and *before* a veritable battalion was on-site and ordered to recover the massive amount of whatever-it-was. They were Major Jesse Marcel, the intelligence-officer of the 509th Bomb Group at Roswell; Captain Sheridan Cavitt, of the Counter-Intelligence Corps; and CIC Master Sergeant Lewis S. "Bill" Rickett. All three were at ground-zero. They all saw the wreckage. Years later Marcel would open up wide on the matter of the debris he saw and collected. Cavitt and Rickett may have seen *more* than debris. *Way* more. Possibly bodies, strange bodies. Brazel and little Dee may have seen one or more of those bodies too.

When the media revealed the weather-balloon explanation, something amazing happened: Roswell was largely, and very quickly, forgotten. Granted, those implicated in the affair never forgot what they saw and experienced. But the media certainly moved on to other things. Plus, back in 1947 there were no UFO research groups around to look into the case. The result? Aside from a few, occasional, brief references in books and magazines in the 1950s and 1960s, Roswell was for all intents and purposes dead and buried – which is precisely how those charged with keeping the disturbing secret wanted it. Things changed, however, in the mid-to-late 1970s. Both William Moore and Stanton Friedman were eagerly pursuing the Roswell story by then; it was a story that was slowly but surely destined to be resurrected. It was Friedman who found the now-elderly Jesse Marcel. The long-retired major had a most interesting story to tell:

> "I saw a lot of wreckage but no complete machine. It had disintegrated before it hit the ground. The wreckage was scattered over an area about three quarters of a mile long and several hundred feet wide. I was pretty well acquainted with most everything that was in the air at that time, both ours and foreign. I was also acquainted with virtually every type of weather-balloon or radar-tracking device being used by either the civilians or the military. What it was we didn't know. We just picked up the fragments…it certainly wasn't anything built by us."

Mack Brazel's son, Bill, would later say that what was found on the Foster Ranch was "...something on the order of tinfoil except that [it] wouldn't tear...You could wrinkle it and lay it back down and it immediately resumed its original shape. Quite pliable, but you couldn't crease or bend it like ordinary metal. Almost like a plastic, but definitely metallic in nature."

When Friedman spoke with Bill Rickett, in 1985, the also-long-retired Counter-Intelligence Corps man revealed a few snippets of information on what happened, but practically froze like a deer caught in headlights when Friedman brought up the matter of bodies. It was clearly an issue Rickett had no intention of discussing – and he didn't.

As for Sheridan Cavitt, he proved to be one of the trickiest players in the entire story. He revealed very little of substance. On occasion, he even denied having ever been at Roswell or at the crash site. Cavitt may even have withheld what he knew of the incident when, in 1994, the Air Force came knocking on his front-door, wanting answers – as will become clear later on.

Since the days of the late 1970s and the 1980s, Roswell has risen to stratospheric proportions. Researchers Kevin Randle, Don Schmitt, and Tom Carey have all investigated the mystery to significant degrees. They continue to do so. The Air Force and the Government Accountability Office have both published reports on the case. Numerous non-fiction books and novels, television documentaries, and a movie have been made on the world famous affair. The number of people who have spoken out about their knowledge of what happened – whether first-, second-, or third-hand – is now well into the *hundreds*. People talk of dead aliens, preserved corpses, the back-engineering of alien artifacts found on the Foster Ranch, secret files on the case, old B&W photographs

taken at the crash site, and more – including even s
People murdered to keep the truth hidden? Maybe, y
really could be that high – even decades later.

The end for Roswell is nowhere in sight. Like
Tokyo-trashing Godzilla, it's an indestructible colossus. C
Perhaps, Roswell is finally verging on collapse – at least, in t
of it being perceived as an extraterrestrial event.

Welcome to the latest news on the Roswell-themed story
that UFOlogy hates and which, back in 2005, made me public
enemy number one.

Nick Redfern, May 2017

1:

SOMETHING CRASHES AND A STORY BREAKS

NUMEROUS pro-UFO books have been written on that certain, controversial incident which occurred on the Foster Ranch in early July 1947. It has become far better known as the Roswell UFO crash. Those aforementioned books include *Roswell in the 21st Century* by Kevin Randle, *The Children of Roswell* by Tom Carey and Don Schmitt, *The Roswell Incident* by Charles Berlitz and William Moore, *The UFO Crash at Roswell* by Kevin Randle and Don Schmitt, and *Crash at Corona* by Stanton Friedman and Don Berliner. As for the U.S. Air Force, it has now published two reports on Roswell – one in 1994 and the other in 1997. Neither report endorses the alien angle, which should surprise absolutely no-one. The conclusion of the USAF, today, is that the Roswell wreckage came not from a weather-balloon, as was claimed by the Air Force way back in July 1947, but from a huge "Mogul" balloon-array utilized to secretly monitor for Soviet atomic bomb tests in the latter part of the 1940s. As for the reports of alien bodies found at the crash site, it is the Air Force's firm opinion that they were crash-test-dummies used in high-altitude parachute experiments. There is, however, another theory for what happened outside of Roswell in early July 1947. In some ways, it's a theory that is *more* controversial than the idea that aliens crashed and died on the ranch.

The Foster Ranch: Roswell's "Ground Zero" (Nick Redfern)

* * * * * * * * * * *

WELCOME TO THE JUNGLE

In June 2005, Simon & Schuster published what is without doubt the most controversial book I have ever written. Its title: *Body Snatchers in the Desert: The Horrible Truth at the Heart of the Roswell Story*. It's a book which suggested that what crashed outside of Roswell, New Mexico in early July 1947 was not an alien spacecraft, after all, but one of a handful of definitively *terrestrial* vehicles which were secretly test-flown by the U.S. military in various parts of New Mexico. And, all over the course of several months in the year in which (a) the flying saucer was born, (b) the CIA was created, and (c) the passing of the National Security Act went ahead. We're talking about 1947. All of the flights ended in disaster, and particularly so for the people on-board. This was something which ensured that the tales, revelations and rumors of more than a few "crashed flying saucers and dead aliens," in the Land of

Enchantment, and in the late-1940s, became intertwined and confused. To the extent that they are now popularly recognized under one banner, that of the "the Roswell incident."

The overwhelming secrecy surrounding the flights was due to the fact that certain controversy-filled pacts had secretly been put into place. They were designed to allow a large number of German and Japanese scientists to avoid prosecution for their Second World War-era war-crimes. Instead, those scientists secretly went to work for the U.S. Government – and that included working on the craft that crashed to earth outside of Roswell, New Mexico and which led to the infamous legend of the UFO crash. Some of those craft were piloted. Others had human guinea-pigs on board – handicapped people – who were strapped into gondolas and lifted high into the sky by huge balloon arrays, chiefly to further expand the scope of controversial work in the field of high-altitude exposure and early rocketry.

In other words, had the truth of Roswell surfaced back then, the floodgates would almost certainly have opened wide, and the sinister treaty - with ardent Nazis and crazed Japanese scientists who had no qualms at all about using innocent people in nightmarish experiments - would have reared its ugly head. No-one in officialdom wanted that to happen, so it was a case of burying the dark and disturbing truth of the diabolical human experimentation among a mass of tales of aliens from other worlds, flying saucers, dummies, and spy-balloons. Destroy all of the records. Deny everything that needs denying. Silence those who know too much. Create as many false leads as possible. Couldn't be done? As I write these words in 2017, I can say with confidence that that approach has worked all too well for the last seventy years. As for the timeline that my 2005 book described, it went like this:

* * * * * * * * * * *

A SECRET HISTORY

During the latter stages of the Second World War, the Japanese military is working to perfect highly advanced balloons as weapons of war – to the extent that on June 4, 1945, a Japanese military spokesman states that their so-called Fugo balloon launches of the previous few months – balloons equipped with bombs and which result in a small number of fatalities on American soil - are merely the precursors for something far more dangerous, including large-scale attacks. The new balloons will be piloted by "death-defying" Japanese military personnel.

The new balloons, American experts estimate, will be at least sixty feet in diameter and will be able to carry a pressurized gondola containing four relatively small men to a height of around 30,000 feet as the balloons travel upon their stratospheric, four-day flights across the Pacific to the United States. Similarly, declassified FBI, CIA, Air Force and British Government memoranda reveals that in the same time frame, the Germans are actively pursuing several new and novel aviation-based projects, including the construction of circular- and elliptical-shaped aircraft – a number of which are based upon the groundbreaking work of Walter and Reimar Horten, aviation geniuses who worked for the Nazis on a number of revolutionary aircraft designs.

In addition, extensive wartime research is conducted by the Japanese Government's Unit 731 – which performed unforgivable medical atrocities on captured people - and by Nazi scientists in the extremely controversial area of human experimentation. A large body of that same experimentation is devoted to better understanding the effects of high-altitude exposure on human beings and is undertaken, in part, on physically handicapped individuals.

At the close of hostilities, scientific, aviation and medical experts from Japan and Germany are secretly brought to the United States – via a secret project called Paperclip and its Japanese equivalent – where human experimentation and advanced aircraft research continues unabated and under just about the strictest security possible. President Clinton's Advisory Committee on Human Radiation Experiments notes in the 1990s: "At least 1,600 scientists and their dependents were recruited and brought to the United States by Paperclip and its successor projects through the early 1970s."

The committee continues:

> "The ACHRE also notes with respect to the time period in question that a number of potentially important collections could not be located and were evidently lost or destroyed. Similarly, the Committee reveals, a number of those same document collections related to experiments undertaken in the fields of biomedicine, defense and space exploration; and in the great majority of these cases only fragmentary data remained. Where programs were legitimately kept secret for national security reasons, states the Committee, the government often did not create or maintain adequate records, thereby preventing the public, and those most at risk, from learning the facts in a timely and complete fashion."

In the aftermath of the War, a number of military research sites recruit Paperclip scientists with backgrounds in aero-medicine, radiobiology and ophthalmology. Those sites include the Air Force's School of Aviation Medicine - from where experiments into total-body irradiation, space medicine, space biology and flash-blindness are undertaken - and the New Mexico-based White Sands Proving Ground. The latter becomes home to the V2 rockets developed by – and captured from - Nazi Germany during the War.

In addition, at the same time that the Paperclip personnel are actively being brought to the United States, the Air Force's Aero Medical Center gives its top priority to the translation of manuscripts providing a complete picture of German aviation medicine.

Further advances are made in the field of aviation in post-war America: the Air Force awards to the Fairchild Engine and Airplane Corporation a contract that establishes Fairchild as the responsible agency of the NEPA nuclear aircraft project; and the Holloman Balloon Branch, Holloman Air Force Base, New Mexico, eventually goes on to become a recognized component of the space-race, via its involvement in what is known as the Discoverer program.

Then, on July 1, 1947 – just a couple of days before the Foster Ranch incident happened - Major Curtis E. LeMay, Major General, U.S. Army, Deputy Chief of Air Staff for Research and Development, orders that research into the biological effects of radiation on Japanese individuals should begin.

* * * * * * * * * * *

CONTROVERSIAL EXPERIMENTATION

In the summer of 1947 and against this backdrop of (a) secret tests on human subjects, (b) revolutionary aircraft- and secret balloon-based programs, and (c) an influx of senior scientific, medical and aviation experts into the United States from Japan and Germany, a series of events and accidents occur on and near the White Sands Proving Ground, New Mexico, which lead to the deliberate creation of cover-stories concerning crashed saucers and dead E.T.s. Witnesses at several crash sites report seeing the remains of unusual-looking aircraft and small bodies, some with enlarged bald heads and Asian or "Oriental"-like features.

On August 19, 1947, FBI Special Agent S.W. Reynolds informs the Bureau's director, J. Edgar Hoover, that in a meeting with a Lieutenant Colonel George D. Garrett, the latter expresses his firm belief that "the flying discs" originate with a highly classified experiment of the Army or Navy. Alien they are not, the FBI is told.

In the immediate wake of the Roswell affair, Dr. Lincoln LaPaz of the University of New Mexico – and a wartime expert on the Fugo balloons, no less – becomes deeply embroiled in the Roswell controversy; the ramifications of the Nuremberg Code begin to reverberate and rumble within the United States; and, as the November 3, 1947 issue of the *Biology Division Bulletin* of the Clinton National Laboratory reveals staff take an active interest in experimentation undertaken to determine the effect of radioactive iodine on dwarfs and those afflicted with Progeria - a syndrome that results in a small stature, an enlarged, bald-head and on occasion extra fingers and toes – go ahead.

Add to that the testimony of a number of elderly whistleblowers who I interviewed extensively in the early 2000s, and who chose to reveal the absolute darkest side of post-war history and secrecy, and what you have is the story told in my book. Terrible and wholly unethical experiments rather than the bad flying skills of extraterrestrials, were at the heart of what many believe to be the most important UFO case of all.

At the time I write this new book, the interviews conducted with my elderly sources began sixteen years ago, and more than a decade has now gone by since the book was published. Those sources were Al Barker, Bill Salter (both of whom worked in the field of intelligence and espionage and who were in their early eighties when I spoke with them), a retired military man who I referred to as the Colonel, and an elderly woman I called the Black Widow, and who was in her late seventies when I interviewed her in the summer of 2001. In the period since *Body Snatchers in the Desert* surfaced and provoked a wealth of anger, dismay and even – in some quarters – shattered dreams and crushed hopes, far more relevant information has surfaced. The picture it paints is decidedly bleak. It adds significantly to what we know of Roswell and what occurred, rather than what so many want to believe or wish happened, on that famous day back in July 1947.

A couple more, final things for the Introduction...

I didn't just write this book to share with you the latest news on the story that suggests aliens *didn't* crash at Roswell. I also wrote it to correct some significant misconceptions. For example, when *Body Snatchers in the Desert* surfaced, time and time again I saw it referred to as "Nick Redfern's theory," or as "Nick Redfern's story." The implication was that I was the only one who was looking into this particular angle – or who had *ever* looked into it. This was, however, a major misrepresentation of the facts. People *still* repeat that mistake today.

Part of the reason why I have chosen to write the sequel to *Body Snatchers in the Desert* is to demonstrate that – contrary to what some might say - numerous people and sources within UFOlogy have uncovered near-identical data to that which I was exposed to. In that sense, I am far from being a lone wolf. There is an entire pack of us.

Lastly, if you are completely new to my books, by now you may well think I am a UFO skeptic; I can totally see why you might think that. But, I'm not a UFO skeptic; *not* in the slightest. I have seen enough, heard enough, experienced enough, and investigated enough to know that there is a very real UFO phenomenon in our midst. It is a phenomenon that is deeply interested in us, as a species, but which is determined to remain steadfastly in the shadows. Yes, UFOs are real. I just don't think one crashed in the U.S. southwest in the summer of 1947.

2:

WHOSE ROSWELL TRUTH IS THE REAL ROSWELL TRUTH?

ALTHOUGH there is an almost accepted assumption that Roswell either involved a spacecraft from another world or a Mogul balloon of the U.S. military, the fact is that there are more than *a dozen* explanations for what happened - and that's even without the "human experiment" angle added to the mix. I mention this to demonstrate that, regardless of your personal opinion on the story this book tells, Roswell is nowhere near as resolved as many pro-E.T. champions would have you believe. As you'll now see.

* * * * * * * * * * *

"AN ACCIDENT INVOLVING A B-29"

The late Jim Keith was the author of a number of conspiracy / UFO-themed books, including *Casebook on the Men in Black*; *The Octopus* (co-written with Kenn Thomas); and *Black Helicopters Over America*. In a small article titled *Roswell UFO Bombshell*, Keith described his clandestine meeting with "a longtime researcher / instructor of engineering at a school in New Mexico" who claimed to know the truth of Roswell. As for what Keith was told, it goes like this:

> "According to my source, the true story behind the alleged UFO crash was that there was an accident involving a B-29 flying from the Army Air Force Base in Sandia (Albuquerque) to Roswell...my source states that either an atomic bomb or what is termed a 'bomb shape,' or 'test shape,' the shell of a nuke lacking explosives and atomic capability, and sometimes filled with concrete to add weight, was accidentally or purposefully jettisoned above Corona, New Mexico, directly on the flight path between Sandia and Roswell. Along with the bomb, metal foil used for radar jamming, termed 'chaff,' may have also been dropped."

* * * * * * * * * * *

SECRETS OF THE UNDERGROUND

In 2010, Anomalist Books published the final title from the late Mac Tonnies: *The Cryptoterrestrials*. Highly thought-provoking and deeply controversial in equal measures, the book focused on the idea that UFOs are *not* the products of alien races, but of very ancient, terrestrial people that dwell deep underground and who *masquerade* as extraterrestrials to camouflage their true identity.

Tonnies speculated that the Cryptoterrestrials are likely very impoverished, but utilize subterfuge, hologram-style technology, and staged-events to suggest otherwise to us. He even theorized they may have made use of large, balloon-style craft, too. And on this very matter – of the Cryptoterrestrials using balloons in covert missions – Tonnies said: "Maybe the Roswell device wasn't high tech. It could indeed have been a balloon-borne surveillance device brought down in a storm, but it doesn't logically follow that it was one of our own."

* * * * * * * * * * *

COMMIES AND ROSWELL

Annie Jacobsen's book, *Area 51: An Uncensored History of America's Top Secret Military Base*, created a huge wave of controversy when it was published in 2011, and chiefly for one reason. The book includes a story suggesting that the Roswell craft and bodies were, in reality, the diabolical creations of a near-Faustian pact between the notorious Nazi (and "Angel of Death)," Dr. Josef Mengele and Soviet premier, Joseph Stalin.

The purpose of this early Cold War plan, said Jacobsen, was to plunge the United States into a kind of *War of the Worlds*-style panic by trying to convince the U.S. Government that aliens were invading. And how would the plan work? By placing grossly deformed children (courtesy of the crazed Mengele) inside a futuristic-looking aircraft designed by the previously referenced Horten brothers, and then trying to convince the U.S. of the alien origins of both. Unfortunately for Stalin – we are told - the plot failed when a storm brought down the craft and its "crew" in the wilds of New Mexico; an event that did not lead to widespread panic, but which instead was hastily covered-up by U.S. military authorities. Later on, you will hear much more about this strange and unlikely affair.

* * * * * * * * * * *

ROSWELL: WHAT THE HELL?

The Collins Elite is a quasi-official group within the U.S. Government that believes the UFO mystery is one of demonic origins. Yes, fork-tails, horns, fiery pits, and maybe even spinning heads and green vomit - those kind of things. It must be stressed that the conclusions of the group were chiefly belief-driven rather than prompted by hard evidence.

One of the conclusions of the group was that Roswell was nothing less than a brilliant Trojan-Horse. For the members of the Collins Elite, deceptive demons had essentially used a kind of "cosmic alchemy" to create both (a) the so-called "memory-metal" found by Mack Brazel on the Foster Ranch, and (b) the curious bodies – or body-parts – also located on the ranch. In other words, Roswell – as perceived by the Collins Elite, at least – was an ingenious ruse, a staged-crash, designed to have us believe vulnerable E.T.s are in our midst, when it's really the all-powerful minions of Satan. Hellfire!

* * * * * * * * * * *

"A V-2 WARHEAD IMPACTED NEAR THE TOWN OF CORONA, NEW MEXICO, ON JULY 4, 1947"

Although no longer active in the UFO community, Timothy Cooper provoked a wealth of controversy in the 1990s "thanks" to an enormous body of allegedly leaked and supposedly highly secret, documentation in his possession. They were documents which covered everything from crashed UFOs to alien autopsies and from sinister deaths in the UFO field to alien viruses. One such document –titled *UFO Reports and Classified Projects* – offers a non-UFO-themed explanation for what occurred at Roswell. The relevant extract reads as follows:

> "One of the projects underway at that time incorporated re-entry vehicles containing radium and other radioactive materials combined with biological warfare agents developed by I.G. Farben for use against allied assault forces in Normandy in 1944. When a V-2 warhead impacted near the town of Corona, New Mexico, on July 4, 1947, the warhead did not explode and it and the deadly cargo lay exposed to the elements which forced the Armed Forces Special Weapons Project to close off the crash site and a cover story was immediately put out that what was discovered was the remains of a radar tracking target suspended by balloons."

* * * * * * * * * * *

DUMMIES IN THE DESERT

When personnel at the Roswell Army Air Field announced, in July 1947, that they had recovered a crashed flying disc, one thing was one hundred percent absent: any mention of bodies. And, needless to say, the body angle was also absent from the hasty follow-up explanation of a weather-balloon recovery. The body angle was also denied in the Air Force's July 1994 report on Roswell (titled *Report of Air Force Research Regarding the Roswell Incident*), as the following extract shows: "It should also be noted here that there was little mentioned in this report about the recovery of the so-called 'alien bodies.' The wreckage was from a Project Mogul balloon. There were no 'alien' passengers therein."

Dummies in the desert? (U.S. Air Force)

Three years later, however, things had changed. In a new document – *The Roswell Report: Case Closed* – it was stated by the Air Force: "'Aliens' observed in the New Mexico desert were probably anthropomorphic test dummies that were carried aloft by U.S. Air Force high altitude balloons for scientific research...The reports of military units that always seemed to arrive shortly after the crash of a flying saucer to retrieve the saucer and 'crew' were actually accurate descriptions of Air Force personnel engaged in anthropomorphic dummy recovery operations."

* * * * * * * * * * *

MANIPULATING TIMELINES

Then there is the matter of time travel. One of those who revealed his thoughts on this particular scenario was Lieutenant Colonel Philip Corso, co-author with William Birnes of the much-debated, championed and denounced UFO-themed book: *The Day after Roswell.* The unusual bodies found within the wreckage of the craft, Corso claimed, were genetically created beings designed to withstand the rigors of space flight, but they were not the actual creators of the UFO itself.

Right up until the time of his death in 1998, Corso speculated on the distinct possibility that the U.S. Government might *still* have no real idea of who constructed the craft, or who genetically engineered the bodies found aboard. Notably, Corso gave much consideration to the idea that the Roswell UFO was a form of time machine, possibly even one designed and built by the denizens of the Earth of a distant future, rather than by the people of a faraway solar-system.

* * * * * * * * * * *

NAZIS AT ROSWELL

Following the defeat of Nazi Germany in 1945, numerous German scientists were brought to the United States via a program called Operation Paperclip. And many of those same scientists went to work at the New Mexico-based White Sands Missile Range (or the White Sands Proving Ground, as it was known back then). This has led to a scenario involving a highly secret program to test-fly radical Nazi aircraft captured after Hitler and his cronies went belly-up.

Someone who has deeply addressed the Nazi/Roswell links is Joseph P. Farrell, the author of *Roswell and the Reich: The Nazi Connection*. Farrell, however, takes things in a decidedly different direction. He concludes the Roswell event was *not* caused by the flight and crash of a German craft flown from White Sands. Rather, Farrell believes that "what crashed may have been representative of an independent postwar Nazi power – an extraterritorial Reich monitoring its old enemy, America..."

* * * * * * * * * * *

SCARING THE SOVIETS

The Flying Saucer was a science-fiction novel published in 1948 and written by Bernard Newman, a man who penned more than a hundred books on subjects including real-life espionage, global politics and current affairs. It was his foray into the weird world of crashed UFOs that was perhaps most notable of all, however.

The book was published just eleven months after the alleged recovery by the U.S. military of a flying saucer in Lincoln County, New Mexico in July 1947. *The Flying Saucer* tells the story of a secret cabal that stages a series of hoaxed UFO crashes, with the express purpose of attempting to unite the world against a deadly alien foe that in reality does not exist.

That Newman had numerous, high-level connections to officialdom has given rise to the theory that (a) Roswell was, itself, a staged event – one designed to scare the Soviets into thinking the United States had acquired alien technology; and (b) Newman based his "novel" on data secured by sources with top secret knowledge of the Roswell ruse.

* * * * * * * * * * *

THE APES OF ROSWELL

In an article titled *Roswell Explained – Again* (which was published in *Fate* magazine in September 2005), Kevin Randle stated that during the early part of the 1990s, he "interviewed a man who worked with NASA at the White Sands Missile Range." The man in question was Gerald Brown.

Randle continued that Brown speculated "some kind of flying wing had crashed while carrying five chimps dressed in silver flying suits." So far, no evidence has surfaced to suggest that the alien body stories can be explained away via the chimpanzee scenario. On the other hand, there is no hard undeniable evidence for *any* theory when it comes to Roswell.

* * * * * * * * * * *

A SECRET SPY-BALLOON

On July 28, 1995, a report surfaced from the National Security and International Affairs Division of the General Accounting Office (today called the Government Accountability Office) that disclosed the results of its investigation of the Roswell affair. Commenting on an Air Force report on Roswell published in July 1994, the GAO noted the following:

> "DOD informed us that the U.S. Air Force report of July 1994, entitled *Report of Air Force Research Regarding the Roswell Incident*, represents the extent of DOD records or information concerning the Roswell crash. The Air Force report concluded that there was no dispute that something happened near Roswell in July 1947 and that all available official materials indicated the most likely source of the wreckage recovered was one of the project MOGUL balloon trains. At the time of the Roswell crash, project MOGUL was a highly classified U.S. effort to determine the state of Soviet nuclear weapons research using balloons that carried radar reflectors and acoustic sensors."

And that's where things stand to this very day. They are theories that range from the plausible to the unlikely, and with others hazily hovering somewhere in between. A few of those scenarios may be the work of hoaxers or "Walter Mitty"-types. Others – probably most of them - are almost certainly born out of the clandestine worlds of disinformation and psychological warfare. Somewhere, in this confusing mass (and mess) of theories, the truth of Roswell exists.

You may be of the opinion that E.T.s crashed at Roswell. Certainly, that's the dominating theory within UFOlogy. I'm here, however, to point you in another direction.

3:

THE WHISTLEBLOWERS SURFACE

WHEN, in 2005, *Body Snatchers in the Desert* was published, a number of people asked me questions about the sources of material in the book – four, definitive whistleblowers who provided the bulk of the relevant material. It's important to note that I have, on a few occasions, used unnamed sources in my books. Why? Well, usually because the people in question have no wish to be thrust into the public domain – or they don't want inquiring UFOlogists knocking on their front doors, which is completely understandable. So, anonymity is the order of the day, even though I have to admit that it's not an ideal situation.

Two of the people who spoke to me for my book – the Black Widow and the Colonel - had other reasons for not wanting to reveal too much about themselves: One of those reasons eclipsed all of the rest: *fear.* Fear of the government, fear of some sort of reprisal – even though such a retaliation would, in my opinion, be highly unlikely, as it would only legitimize and confirm their claims. Nevertheless, that fear never, ever left them: it was so obviously ever-present when the interviews were conducted. Fortunately, their decisions to reveal what they knew – along with their consciences – outweighed that fear.

For the most part, *Body Snatchers in the Desert* presented the data that the sources shared. What the book did *not* do to any significant degree, however, was to explain how and under what circumstances I got to know all four. Now that they are all gone, it's a good time to expand on the sources and how, exactly, we all crossed paths.

Before we do that, however, it's worth understanding why I am willing to listen to whistleblowers and not write them off. Many people assume that whistleblower data cannot be validated or is worthless. Wrong. Dead wrong. I could provide you with many examples, but for our purposes (and space), I will share with you just one perfect example.

* * * * * * * * * * *

THE RELIABILITY OF UNNAMED SOURCES

Certain people in UFOlogy were highly skeptical when, in 2006, my then-new-book, *On the Trail of the Saucer Spies*, was published and revealed something startling. In the book, I mentioned that a retired British police source (who I referred to as the Sandman), told me that back in the 1990s, the British Police Force's elite Special Branch had opened secret files on two UFO researchers in the U.K. They were Matthew Williams and Robin Cole. When it came to that skepticism, those same certain people should have kept their mouths firmly shut.

The files on Cole and Williams (or rather *some* of the files; others still remain classified to this day) were finally officially released in 2012, showing that Special Branch was indeed watching both men in the 1990s. This demonstrated to me that the data provided seven years earlier by the Sandman was one hundred percent accurate.

When, in 2012, the documents were declassified, the following statement concerning their contents was prepared for the National Archives:

> "File DEFE 24/1984/1 (p294) contains a 1996 Parliamentary Question from Martin Redmond MP [Member of Parliament] asking on how many occasions MI6 and GCHQ have monitored UFO investigations. This was interpreted to mean 'have the agencies been keeping watch on UFOlogists.' A background briefing says 'neither agency in fact undertakes such activity, though GCHQ cannot rule out the possibility' they had monitored in other contexts individuals who have made a study of UFOs.' The MP was told the government do not comment on the intelligence and security agencies (p298). File DEFE 24/1987/1 (p262-65) reveals that in 1997 Special Branch took an interest in a UFOlogist who became obsessed with rumors of a secret UFO facility beneath RAF Rudloe Manor in Wiltshire. The base had become known as the British equivalent of the secret U.S. military airbase 'Area 51' among conspiracy theorists. An internal note said 'Special Branch...do not believe he poses a threat to security, but they are alert to the risk that others may use him as a conduit for their activities.'"

Well, since the summary failed to note the names of the people in question, I will. They were, of course, Cole and Williams - as I had been told years earlier during the course of writing *On the Trail of the Saucer Spies.*

Back in 1997, Robin Cole, of Cheltenham, England - the home to GCHQ (the Government Communications Headquarters) - wrote a fascinating report on the agency's involvement in the UFO phenomenon. And, for those who may not be aware,

GCHQ is the U.K. equivalent of the United States' National Security Agency. You know: Snowden's old stomping grounds.

After Cole's report was published, he was visited by two representatives of the U.K.'s Special Branch. And, since the pair announced their visit in advance (via a phone-call), Robin had the good sense to clandestinely and quickly set up his tape-recorder in his living-room and taped the *entire* conversation, much of which revolved around Special Branch's interest in a UFO researcher and Crop Circle maker named Matthew Williams - who just happens to be the "UFOlogist who became obsessed" with RAF Rudloe Manor, as referenced by the National Archives.

Special Branch's concerns, the documentation reveals, were that both the UFO controversy and the people that investigate it could be used as tools of manipulation by hostile groups with controversial, political agendas. Every aspect of the story told to me off-the-record between 2004 and 2006 by the Sandman was vindicated when the National Archives made available the relevant files in 2012.

That's just one of the reasons why I don't dismiss UFO-related data provided by sources who prefer to lurk in the shadows, but who are also willing to divulge what they know, even if their names aren't revealed. Now, back to the other whistleblowers, the ones who shared with me what they knew about Roswell.

* * * * * * * * * * *

OLD SECRETS SURFACE

Back in 1998, I wrote a book titled *The FBI Files*. It told the story of the Bureau's involvement in the UFO phenomenon, contactee cases, the alleged Aztec, New Mexico UFO crash of 1948, the cattle mutilation mystery, and even FBI records on the sinister *Men in Black*. Chapter Four of the book was titled "The Oak Ridge Invasion." As so often happens when I write a book, people who personally know something of its contents or subject-matter will contact me and share the relevant information. And that is precisely what happened with regard to that chapter. It was a study of FBI files that had been declassified under the terms of the Freedom of Information Act and which described various UFO encounters at the Oak Ridge National Laboratory, Tennessee, from the late 1940s to the early 1950s.

One of the people who contacted me – by letter, via the London, England-based publisher of *The FBI Files*, Simon & Schuster - was an elderly woman who worked at Oak Ridge in 1947, and who had read my book. She added she had some information that I was sure to find of interest, but which she preferred to tell me about in person. Well, as I was living in the U.K. at that time, there wasn't much of a chance of me meeting up with her at any time soon – which is exactly what I told her. I couldn't persuade her to put her revelations onto paper. Nor would she share them with me over the telephone. And, she wasn't on email – not a massive number of old folks were online in 1998, I am guessing. So, for a couple of years it was a case of her story not just stalling, but coming to a complete halt. That is, until the summer of 2001.

* * * * * * * * * * *

LUNCH WITH A WIDOW

I moved to the United States to live in early 2001, and, in the summer, I traveled around much of the west coast – chiefly to do a series of lectures for various UFO groups in California. I put out a feeler to that same old lady, explaining my new circumstances and asking if we could now, finally, talk. Well, that would be just fine, she said. On July 28, 2001 I hung out with the then-seventy-nine-year-old woman: we had lunch in a Los Angeles restaurant and chatted extensively. She was driven to the restaurant by a family member, a much younger man who seemed to be equally as worried as she was. Nevertheless, she agreed to share what she knew, providing her name was never published (although, she was required to provide Simon & Schuster's legal people with a release-form, as were each and all of the other whistleblowers). So, I sat back and listened.

I referred to her in the book as the Black Widow. There was a relevant reason for this; a reason which was not mentioned in *Body Snatchers in the Desert*: her husband, who she married in 1972, was African-American. She, however, was not. They were both just into their very early fifties when they married and had twenty-four happy years together, despite some unforgivable racist comments from her ignorant family. It was in 1996 that her husband passed away, hence the title I gave her.

When we met, and knowing that she had read *The FBI Files*, my natural assumption was that she wanted to tell me something about UFO encounters at the Oak Ridge facility. Makes sense, right? No. I was wrong: what she actually wanted to share with me was certain information that, if provable, would radically alter the face of UFOlogy and blow the Roswell case right out of the water. As we ate, I wondered, with a fair degree of excitement: what the hell have I got myself into? It wasn't long before I had the answer to that loaded question.

The Black Widow, born in 1922, had been in the employ of Oak Ridge from the mid-1940s to the early 1950s. While there, and on three occasions between May and July 1947, she saw a number of unusual-looking bodies brought to the facility – and under stringent security. They looked like regular Japanese people, she said. Others, however, displayed the signs of certain medical conditions: dwarfism, oversized heads, and bulging eyes. A few of the bodies were extensively damaged – as if they had been in violent accidents, which proved to be the case. In all, fifteen such bodies were brought to Oak Ridge under great secrecy; all of them reportedly used in certain high-altitude, balloon-based experiments in New Mexico, one of which led to the Roswell legend. Or, became a part of the legend is probably more correct. The Black Widow said: "Those bodies – the Roswell bodies – they weren't aliens. The government could care less about those stories about alien bodies found at Roswell – except to hide the truth."

She added: "I don't know anything at all about how these people were brought [to the United States], but I heard at Oak Ridge that some of them were in the States in late 1945 and brought over with Japanese doctors and Nazi doctors who had been doing similar experiments. That's when some of this began."

The story continued that at least some of the people used in the tests were American prisoners given the opportunity to cut the lengths of their sentences – if, that is, they were willing to take a chance and take part in the dicey experiments. Reportedly, a number did take the bait, but failed to survive the flights. Some of the handicapped people did not come from Japan, but from "hospitals and asylums" in the United States.

All of the material evidence was said to have been eventually destroyed – chiefly because the operations didn't provide much in the way of results, and because of the outright illegality of the experiments. Everything, the Black Widow said, was hidden beneath a mass of fabricated tales of flying saucers and little men from the stars. She doubted that anything of any significance still existed – certainly not the bodies or the balloons, and probably not even the old records, which she believed were burned to oblivion. Unless, however, some of them were preserved for secret, historical purposes, which is not impossible. I hope they were. If not, it may be nigh on impossible to conclusively prove *anything* about Roswell – ever.

* * * * * * * * * * * *

SILENCING THOSE WHO SAW THE BODIES

There was one other aspect of the Black Widow's story that needs to be addressed: her overwhelming fear. It was ever-present throughout our 2001 meeting. She tried to disguise that fear with smiles and laughter, but she was certainly no Oscar-winning Hollywood actor. That's for sure. Seeing through her façade was like seeing through freshly polished glass. In *Body Snatchers in the Desert* I said that she "possessed the sad and somewhat sunken eyes of a person with the weight of the world on her shoulders. She was clearly looking for someone to speak with; but, equally, she was very concerned about the ramifications of doing so, 'if the government finds out.'"

In my original manuscript, I detailed why she was so scared, but that section didn't make the cut. The reason? The publisher was highly concerned about the Black Widow's claims to me that certain people who had got too close to the truth of Roswell, and who couldn't keep their mouths shut, had been...*murdered by the government.* So the story went, certain hired assets, who regularly worked with the intelligence community on "troublesome" situations, were secretly contracted to terminate those who threatened the status quo and its dangerous secret. Interestingly, the Black Widow made a mention to me of a long-retired nurse from Roswell who had died under extremely questionable circumstances "a few years ago." I didn't know it at the time, but it's highly possible that she was referring to a woman named Miriam Bush.

Miriam was not actually a nurse: in 1947 she was an executive secretary at Roswell's RAAF hospital. She worked for a medical officer, Lieutenant Colonel Harold Warne, and saw the bodies found on the Foster Ranch – when they were brought into the confines of the hospital. They were, as nearly everyone claimed, small, damaged, and unusual-looking. This trauma-filled experience clearly affected Miriam to a huge degree. The whole thing was like an albatross around her neck. That huge, ominous bird never left her.

Miriam's private life was a mess and she became alcoholic – as did, by the way, both Major Jesse Marcel and Dee Proctor; a sign, perhaps of the tremendous burden of hiding what they may have known. And, in the late 1980s, Miriam became fearful that she was being watched and followed. *She was.* Miriam Bush was found dead in a motel-room just outside of San Jose, California, in

December 1989. A plastic bag was around her head and her arms were bruised and scratched. The verdict? Suicide. Yeah, really.

When the story of Miriam Bush surfaced - years after I spoke with the Black Widow, and also a couple of years after *Body Snatchers in the Desert* was published – my mind instantly swung back to the Black Widow's comments relative to the highly suspicious death of a certain "nurse" from Roswell. Was it Miriam Bush? I don't know. But, logically, it would make sense.

If so, though, how did the Black Widow know this? After all, Miriam was based at Roswell, New Mexico and the Black Widow worked in Tennessee. I have no answer to that question; I wish I did. But, I do know that the Black Widow's major concern about speaking on the record was the fear that she would finish up like the woman from Roswell; a woman who happened to be in the wrong place at the wrong time, and who paid for it with her life, years later.

* * * * * * * * * * *

FEAR OF THE BODIES

The story of Miriam Bush and the words of the Black Widow led me to conclude that those who saw the bodies – and who might still be in positions to reveal what they knew – were the ones who had far more to fear and lose than anyone else. After all, seeing – and even handling – the debris all those years ago wasn't really a big cause of concern for those in government who were determined to keep the secret hidden. Accounts of odd-looking foil couldn't prove anything conclusive. Such accounts *still* can't prove anything. But, credible people attached to the military and the government and who saw the corpses – like the Black Widow and like Miriam Bush – had everything to lose. Including their lives.

Sheridan Cavitt and Bill Rickett knew enough to avoid discussing the angle of bodies wherever, and whenever, possible. Dee Proctor, as a young boy, had the fear of God put in him by the military – and to such an extent that he never ever brought up the word *bodies*. But Miriam Bush did share her story. And something happened in late 1989 that upped the ante and led to her death. Little wonder, then, that the Black Widow also had a deep fear that she too would be killed. Like Miriam, she saw the bodies. Later on we'll see how yet another source who saw the bodies, Dr. Lejeune Foster, was also told that if she ever spoke out on what she knew her life would be over.

Since the bodies, or even just one of them, would be the prime piece of evidence that could prove the true nature of the Roswell event – human or extraterrestrial - it makes perfect sense that those who were in positions to reveal what they knew would potentially be the most dangerous of all to the secret-keepers.

* * * * * * * * * * * *

"1 WAS SUSPECTED OF PROGERIA...FOUR WERE DWARFS"

On the matter of the Black Widow seeing unusual bodies at Oak Ridge, it is worth noting that the November 3, 1947 edition of the *Biology Division Bulletin* of Oak Ridge's Clinton National Laboratory contains a paper titled "Current Journal Articles of Interest in the Biology Library." One of those same articles was focused on research into children with thyroid-based disorders. It was written by Edith H. Quimby and Donovan McCune, M.D., in August 1947. The article, along with other documents from Oak Ridge, reveals that staff at the facility had undertaken research on "...fifty-four test subjects." Those same "test subjects" were comprised of "...fifteen [who] were between one and four years of age; 7 were controls; 2 were classic cretins; 1 showed some features of hypothyroidism which were not modified by treatment; 2 were dwarfs; in 1 the diagnosis was 'gargoylism;' 1 was suspected of Progeria, a disorder associated with some of the features of hypothyroidism; and the last exhibited features of moderate sexual precocity. Twenty-seven were more than four but less than fifteen years of age. Of these 2 had unmistakable hypothyroidism, 2 Graves disease, four were dwarfs."

This is, of course, decidedly interesting. Barely a month after Roswell, people displaying evidence of both dwarfism and Progeria (the latter a condition resulting in small stature, a lack of body hair, and an over-sized head) were taken to Oak Ridge; to personnel at the Biology Division who were expressing "interest" in their conditions.

But, there's more. One would expect that the documentation cited above would only have been of interest to the medical community. Not so...

On digging further, I was able to uncover the fact that these same files on individuals with dwarfism and Progeria were shared with (a) staff from the Nuclear Energy for Propulsion of Aircraft program (NEPA); and (b) one William Randolph Lovelace II, who lived in Albuquerque, New Mexico and who, in the 1930s and '40s, worked on high-altitude exposure issues relative to the human body (some in conjunction with staff at Wright Field - now Wright-Patterson Air Force Base, Dayton Ohio.) In 1958,

Lovelace was appointed the chairman of the NASA Special Advisory Committee on Life Science.

Lovelace also had a startling connection to the Roswell crash, as will be revealed in a later chapter.

Now, back to the whistleblowers.

* * * * * * * * * * *

MORE SOURCES COME OUT OF THE SHADOWS

I sat back and took in the tale of the Black Widow. It was, to be sure, a controversial story. But, that wasn't the end of it. As I mentioned to the late English UFO researcher Stuart Miller in the latter part of 2005 – for an extensive interview which appeared in his online *UFO Review* magazine - the Black Widow was acquainted with three other people who also knew a great deal about all of this. Admittedly, and unfortunately, the precise nature of the connection was something I was never able to fully figure out. And the Black Widow didn't want to say too much on this particular matter, anyway. It was a case of take it or leave it. I took it.

Two of the three were Bill Salter and Al Barker, who I met on several occasions, almost always in out-of-the-way southwest diners and at the times and places of their choosing. They had worked in the 1950s in the fields of counter-intelligence and psychological warfare and were already octogenarians when I spoke with them in the early-2000s. Neither man was ever at Roswell, but secured their data on the case – and on the various other 1945-1947 events – from files they read in the fifties. They were adamant that not a single extraterrestrial ever visited, flew over, or died in, New Mexico. In 1947, or at any other time. But, they both stressed, a number of unfortunate *people* did die, and their deaths were hastily hidden. Huge balloons, lifting-body-type craft, and sacrificed souls were the key ingredients.

Then, there was the Colonel – another man who claimed deep knowledge of what happened at Roswell, of Japanese balloons, of human experiments of a very controversial nature, and of much more that suggested aliens did not crash at Roswell. He too had a link to the Black Widow; a link that was never unraveled fully. But, the Colonel assured me that he had read files in the 1960s that detailed the human nature of the Roswell affair. Extensive interviews were undertaken with all four – and which made their way into the heart of *Body Snatchers in the Desert.*

Oddly, for all the shouting, screaming, and the occasional shrill yapping of certain Roswell investigators in the UFO research community, not a single one of them ever asked me if I could put them in touch with my sources, or if I could forward an email or a message on to them. What did those same researchers think I was going to do? Bite their heads off? The thought did cross my mind. Maybe that same community was fearful of what it might have found out or heard. Perhaps, an "ignorance is bliss" approach was the only thing they could face dealing with. Maybe so. But, that was not my approach. I followed the story as deeply as I could and I told it in my 2005 book.

Now, in 2017, it's time to reveal more of the story that certain factions of UFOlogy just wish would go away. They probably wish I would go away, too. No chance.

4:

"A VERY HIGHLY CLASSIFIED EXPERIMENT OF THE ARMY"

IF, as my *Body Snatchers in the Desert* book suggested, certain key events in the summer of 1947 – of a *perceived* flying saucer nature – had far less to do with the actions of aliens and far more to do with matters of a classified military nature, then it would be most reasonable to assume that (a) discussions of such a possibility would have been flying around Washington, D.C., and (b) the government, and people in the military, would have been secretly digging deep to try and determine if this was indeed the case. Guess what? That is *exactly* what happened.

Although many UFO investigators have said that the government's worries and concerns about UFOs in '47 were provoked by fear of them having definitive alien or Soviet origins, we have prime evidence in our hands that demonstrates the domestic "secret weapon" angle was one most definitely discussed – and even accepted – at an official level, as we shall now see. It is a crucial part of the argument that at least some UFOs are not from faraway worlds, but from right here.

In early July 1947, Brigadier General George F. Schulgen, who was the Chief of the Requirements Intelligence Branch of Army Air Corps Intelligence, met with Special Agent S.W. Reynolds of the FBI. The purpose: to determine if the Army Air Force could solicit the assistance of the Bureau on a regular basis in its investigation of the growing flying saucer controversy. General

Schulgen advised Reynolds that, "every effort must be undertaken in order to run down and ascertain whether or not the flying discs are a fact and, if so, to learn all about them."

The foremost thought on General Schulgen's mind, at the time, was that the saucers were probably man-made in origin. He had another theory, too, and confided in Special Agent Reynolds that, "the first reported sightings might have been by individuals of Communist sympathies with the view to causing hysteria and fear of a secret weapon."

It was for this reason that the Army Air Force sought the FBI's assistance.

General Schulgen pledged to the FBI "all the facilities of [my] office as to results obtained." He outlined a plan that would involve the FBI in both locating and questioning witnesses to UFO sightings to ascertain whether they were sincere in their statements that they had seen flying saucers, or whether their statements were prompted by personal desire for publicity or subversive reasons. According to declassified FBI files, Schulgen was careful to advise Reynolds too that: "It has been established that the flying discs are not the result of any Army or Navy experiment."

But was that statement the literal truth? Was someone keeping the FBI in the dark?

* * * * * * * * * * *

"SOME NEW FORM OF DEFENSE PERFECTED BY THE AMERICAN MILITARY"

Following the meeting between Schulgen and Reynolds, FBI Director J. Edgar Hoover instructed his agents to begin investigations into flying saucer sightings, in the manner suggested by General Schulgen. As a result of these investigations, on August 15, 1947 the FBI learned of the distinct possibility that the military's involvement in the flying saucer subject extended beyond that of mere observer. In a memorandum to Edward A. Tamm, the FBI Assistant Director, D.M. Ladd of the Bureau's Domestic Intelligence Division wrote the following:

> "The Director advised on August 14, 1947, that the Los Angeles papers were carrying headlines indicating that Soviet espionage agents had been instructed to determine the facts relative to the flying discs. The article carried a Washington date line and indicated that Red espionage agents had been ordered to solve the question of the flying discs, the Russians being of the opinion that this might be *some new form of defense perfected by the American military* [italics mine]. The article further recalled that during the recent war pieces of tin foil had been dropped in the air for the purpose of off-setting the value of radar being used by the enemy forces and that these aluminum discs might be a new development along this line. The Director inquired as to whether the Bureau had any such information."

Suspecting that, if the Russians were snooping around, the saucers just had to be American in origin, Special Agent Reynolds of the FBI's Liaison Section was directed by J. Edgar Hoover to make further inquiries with the Air Force. Answers were sorely needed. Answers came, too. But, they weren't the ones you might expect them to have been.

On August 19, 1947, Reynolds met with a Lieutenant Colonel George D. Garrett and the entire secret weapon issue was discussed frankly and openly, as were the potential consequences should the Bureau uncover details of a top-secret, domestic research-and-development program. Following their very candid exchange, a remarkable memorandum captioned "Flying Discs" was prepared by Reynolds for the attention of Hoover. It is this document, perhaps more than any other, which indicates that the American military was testing flying saucer-type aircraft in the summer of 1947. Or, craft that were not circular-shaped but which still came under the UFO banner, such as massive balloon arrays. The document reads as follows:

* * * * * * * * * * *

"A VERY HIGHLY CLASSIFIED EXPERIMENT OF THE ARMY OR NAVY"

"Special Agent S. W. Reynolds of the Liaison Section, while discussing the above captioned phenomena with Lieutenant Colonel Garrett of the Air Forces Intelligence, expressed the possibility that flying discs were, in fact, a very highly classified experiment of the Army or Navy. Mr. Reynolds was very much surprised when Colonel Garrett not only agreed that this was a possibility, but confidentially stated it was his personal opinion that such was a probability. Colonel Garrett indicated that a Mr. [Deleted], who is a scientist attached to the Air Force's Intelligence, was of the same opinion."

Then, there is this:

> "Colonel Garrett stated that he based his assumption on the following: He pointed out that when flying objects were reported seen over Sweden, the 'high brass' of the War Department extended tremendous pressure on the Air Forces Intelligence to conduct research and collect information in an effort to identify these sightings. Colonel Garrett stated that, in contrast to this, we have reported sightings of unknown objects over the United States, and the 'high brass' appeared to be totally unconcerned. He indicated this led him to believe that they knew enough about these objects to express no concern. Colonel Garrett pointed out further that the objects in question have been seen by many individuals who are what he terms 'trained observers' such as airline pilots. He indicated also that several of the individuals are reliable members of the community. He stated that these individuals saw something. He stated the above has led him to the conclusion that there were objects seen *which somebody in the Government knows all about* [italics mine]."

Special Agent Reynolds then pointed out to the colonel that if flying saucers really *did* originate within the heart of a highly classified domestic project of the military, it was wholly unreasonable for the FBI to be expected to "spend money and precious time conducting inquiries with respect to this matter." The colonel duly concurred with Reynolds; he indicated that it would have been extremely embarrassing to Air Force Intelligence if the saucers proved to be American in origin.

Perhaps sensing that he was now getting very close to uncovering the truth behind the UFO puzzle, Reynolds then made inquiries with the Intelligence Division of the War Department. He wanted their opinion on the theory that something akin to a shadow government operation was responsible for the many flying saucer-type objects seen over North America.

The War Department, however, issued a flat denial that it was in any way implicated in the UFO issue. In a report written up later, Reynolds noted that he was given "the assurance of General Chamberlain and General Todd that the Army is conducting no experiments with anything which could possibly be mistaken for a flying disc."

Nevertheless, the FBI continued to view the subject of flying saucers and the military's involvement in the subject with profoundly suspicious eyes. Rumors continued to circulate within the higher echelons of the FBI that it was being denied access to the full and unexpurgated facts – facts suggesting UFOs were homegrown and not Russian or alien in origin. None of this, of course, proves that the flying saucer wave of the summer of 1947 was provoked by a highly classified military program – rather than one of E.T. origin – but the behind-the-scenes discussions between the likes of Reynolds and Garrett on just such this very possibility most definitely pushed things in that direction.

Also in 1947…

* * * * * * * * * * *

WHEN FLYING SAUCER CRASHES WERE EXPECTED

It's important to note that in the summer of 1947 people were reporting – sometimes hysterically so – crashed saucers all across the United States. Why is that so important? And why is this relevant to Roswell and the story you are now reading? The answer to both questions is simple: if Roswell was the only incident of an alleged flying saucer crash in '47, then a case could indeed be made that it was a unique, one of a kind, event. That there were many such cases, though – all of which turned out to be hoaxes or misidentifications - weakens the case for Roswell as a UFO. Chiefly because, as the following examples show, people were not only reporting crashed saucers in the summer of 1947, there was practically a mindset that *expected* saucers to crash.

When UFO hysteria broke out across the United States, following Kenneth Arnold's famous sighting at Mt. Rainier, people weren't just seeing saucers in the sky. They were finding them all over the place. Almost practically tripping over them. At least, they were until the cases were explained away in simple terms. I won't pummel you with each and every such story, but several of what actually amounts to many will certainly suffice to make the point.

On July 6, 1947, the Portland *Oregonian* reported the following. It has eerie shades of the Roswell story attached to it, with its references to military balloons, tinfoil, a ranch, and even a rancher:

> "Folks in Pickway County, who have been following the 'flying saucer' mystery, became excited Saturday when Sherman Campbell *found a strange object on his farm*

> [italics mine]. It was in the form of a six pointed star, 30 inches high and 48 inches wide, covered with tinfoil. It weighed about two pounds. Attached to the top were the remains of a balloon with a rock 5 inches in circumference. The Fort Columbus airfield weather station at Columbus said the description tallied with an object used by the army air forces to measure wind velocity at high altitudes by the use of radar. Some of the flying discs reported seen in various parts of the country were much larger and flying at terrific speed."

Roswell-like? Yes, very. A crashed spacecraft from another world? Nope.

* * * * * * * * * * *

A SMASHED SAUCER AND AN EVEN MORE SMASHED WITNESS

Moving on twenty-four hours: July 7 was the date on which the *Washington Post* reported the following: "A Catholic priest at Grafton, Wisconsin, said tonight that a round, metal disc, which might be one of the mysterious 'flying saucers,' had crashed into his parish yard and that he is holding it for the Federal Bureau of Investigation."

The source of the story was the Reverend Joseph Brasky who, on the same day, heard what he described as a "swishing and whirring" noise, followed by a thud and a mild explosion. On checking out his yard, Brasky found "a sheet metal disc about 18 inches in diameter, resembling a circular saw blade." The resemblance was not a coincidence: that's exactly what it was.

Given the fact that the *Washington Post* stated that Brasky was waiting for the FBI to get involved, Special Agent H.K. Johnson – who operated out of Milwaukee – looked into the matter and prepared a memorandum. It did not place Brasky in a good light. Johnson recorded that at the time of the event Brasky had been "drinking quite heavily," and despite what he told the *Washington Post*, "Brasky has never contacted the Milwaukee FBI Office or any agent concerning his find. In my opinion, this is just another hoax story, since a photograph of Father Blasky with the saw indicates no basis for any investigation by any authority."

The palaver of the pickled priest was over.

* * * * * * * * * * *

"THIS DISC WOULD NOT BE ABLE TO FLY BY ITSELF"

And, consider the following 1-page FBI report of July 11, 1947, which was sent to the Assistant-to-the-Director Edward A. Tamm. It was yet another "crashed saucer that never was" case, and which was *also* investigated by the aforementioned Special Agent H.K. Johnson. The document states:

> "SAC Johnson of the Milwaukee Office called to advise he had just received a telephone call from [a] Reserve Officer with the Civilian Air Patrol, Black River Falls, Wisconsin. [He] reported that at 3:30 p.m., July 10… at Black River Falls a large 17" disc [was found] which appeared to have been possibly made out of cardboard painted with silver airplane dope. In the center was a tube and a small motor with a propeller attached to the

> side. Colonel [name deleted] expressed the opinion that this disc would not be able to fly by itself. He advised it would be taken to the Air Corps Headquarters."

A wrecked UFO, it was not.

* * * * * * * * * * *

"POSSIBLY THE LINING FROM A JET TURBO PLANE"

I'll share with you one more case which is a bit more intriguing, but which was also shown not to have involved a crashed saucer, after all – despite initial hopes and assumptions. Once again, we turn to the files of the FBI. A teletype message of July 18, 1947, described the discovery of "small burned spots about one and a half inches in diameter on [a] a green lawn [at Rindge, New Hampshire]."

The message continues: "Also in the long dry grass on both sides of road in a circle approximately two hundred feet in diameter several little blazes had started and the Fire Department was called. Fires were apparently caused by metallic fragmentation which were turned over to [the] Massachusetts Institute of Technology."

Although this affair was initially suspected of being one of crashed UFO proportions, a source cited by the FBI stated that the fragments resembled the lining of captured, German V-2 rockets, "which he had observed at New Mexico."

On the other hand, a source at MIT said that the fragments "are possibly the lining from a jet turbo plane." Whatever the answer, the wreckage did not originate with a crashed disc from another planet, as had initially been suspected.

* * * * * * * * * * *

A MONTH OF CRASHED UFO MADNESS

As the examples above show (all of which can be found in the declassified UFO files at the FBI's website, The Vault), in the very same month as Roswell, people were mistaking down-to-earth materials for the remains of crashed saucers, in many other locations across the nation.

In other words, July 1947 was not just a month in which the United States was hit by UFO fever. July 1947 was also the month in which the United States was hit by *crashed* UFO fever. Had Roswell been a one-off example of an alleged UFO crash in July 1947, then I almost certainly wouldn't be writing these words, as it would have been a unique, stand-out event. But that's not what happened: people were reporting crashed saucers all over the place.

Now, I'm not saying that the many and varied bogus tales of crashed UFOs in July 1947 *definitely* have an adverse effect upon Roswell, which occurred in the same month as all those cases above. I do, however, think it's important to recognize that when the Roswell event happened (and in its immediate aftermath), the nation was *already* talking about crashed discs.

That's to say, the time-frame, the media's and the FBI's involvement in claims of crashed discs, the public's mindset, and the context, are all important angles when it comes to the bigger issue of trying to figure out what happened at Roswell - and also why, exactly, the wreckage was perceived as having come from a flying saucer. The fact is that in that crazy month of July 1947, all manner of things were perceived as crashed saucers. But, as the official record demonstrates, they *weren't* crashed saucers.

5:

JAPANESE BALLOONS, ROSWELL, AND THE FBI

AT this stage in the story, I am going to draw your attention to the fact that J. Edgar Hoover's FBI noted a parallel between the investigation of UFOs in the summer of 1947 and the Japanese balloon wave of a few years earlier, when the Second World War was still raging. The FBI document quoted from below – which surfaced thanks to Freedom of Information legislation - shows that in the summer 1947 there was a mindset that suggested "disk" sightings were not unlike the Japanese Fugo balloon sightings and investigations of a couple of years earlier – at least, in terms of how they should be investigated. According to the FBI:

> "It is felt that the situation regarding these flying saucers and flying disks is very similar to the situation which was previously encountered by the Bureau during the past war in handling complaints arising out of the sightings of Japanese balloons. You will recall that at the inception of these complaints the Bureau conducted considerable investigation and located numerous balloons as a cooperative measure for the Army then informed that these were military weapons and that they would take over the handling of these completely. This they did and in an extremely short time issued a big press release as to the splendid work of the Army in locating these Japanese

> balloons. From the information available thus far it does not appear that these disks should be treated other than as a military weapon. Certainly the Bureau has no way to determine what experiments the Army and Navy are conducting and whether such might be arising out of experiments being conducted by them, nor do we have any way of determining how far the Russians have progressed in certain experiments and whether such might be the results of experiments by the Russian Army."

As this memo reveals, the FBI was making certain investigative parallels between the Fugo balloons of the Second World War and the flying saucers of 1947. It is most eye-opening that the FBI also noted: "...the Bureau has no way to determine what experiments the Army and Navy are conducting and whether such might be arising out of experiments being conducted by them..."

This strongly suggests there was a fair degree of belief, or suspicion, within the FBI that what was being seen was not from some faraway star-system, but from right here. On Earth. That the FBI also stated, "From the information available thus far it does not appear that these disks should be treated other than as a military weapon," also speaks volumes about where the collective mind of the FBI was.

In view of what we have seen so far, we can make a good case that in the summer of 1947, the FBI knew – or at least strongly suspected – that UFOs were the product of Uncle Sam. Now, let's take a look at a certain, central figure in the Roswell mystery who also had a link to...*wartime Japanese balloons.*

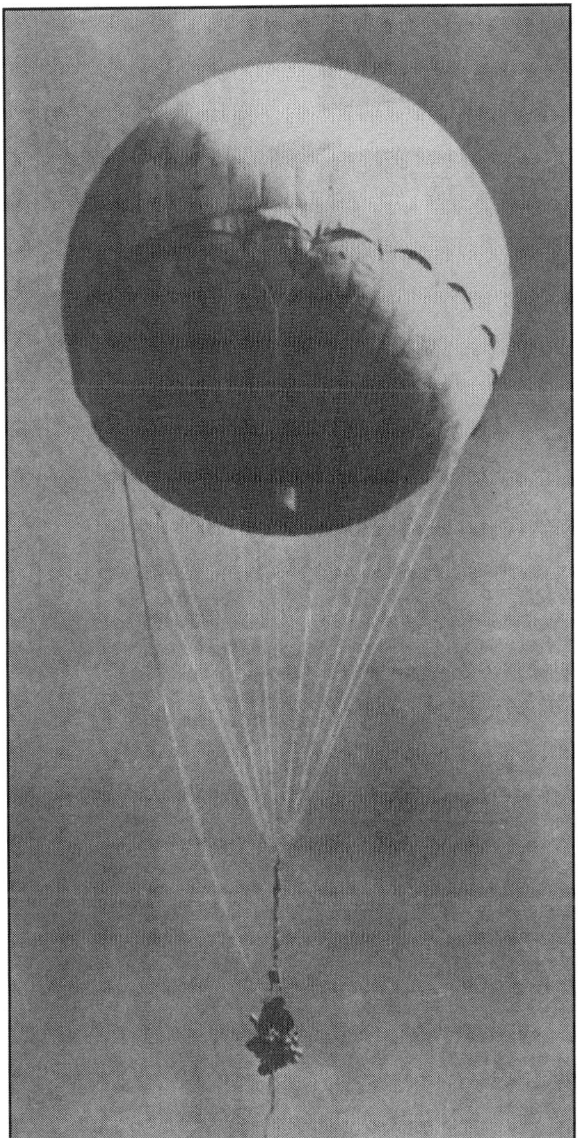

Japan's Fugo Balloon (U.S. Government)

* * * * * * * * * * * *

"CERTAIN SUBJECTS WERE DISCUSSED ONLY IN ROOMS THAT COULDN'T BE BUGGED"

Master Sergeant Lewis "Bill" Rickett – of the Counter-Intelligence Corps (CIC) – was someone who many Roswell investigators believe knew *exactly* what happened on the Foster Ranch in July 1947. At the time of the mysterious event, Rickett was the Non-Commissioned Officer-in-Charge at the Roswell Army Air Field. Years after the event, Rickett admitted to UFO researchers his presence at the ranch site – along with Sheridan Cavitt, also of the CIC - on July 8. Rickett also shared a few other snippets of data, when the mood took him. For the most part, though, he remained very tight-lipped – even cagey at times – on exactly what took place.

Rickett did, however, admit that approximately two months after the crash on the Foster Ranch took place, he liaised on the top secret matter with one Dr. Lincoln LaPaz. At the time, he was the Director of the University of New Mexico's Institute of Meteoritics. He and LaPaz undertook a secret assignment to try and figure out "the speed and trajectory" of the craft that slammed into the heart of Lincoln County. Reportedly, the pair found a "touchdown" location just a few miles from the ranch, as well as a patch of ground that had been exposed to a significant amount of heat. According to Rickett, the object that hurtled to the ground on the ranch was somewhat bat-winged, but certainly not what anyone would call a flying saucer – which is an important point, given that all the talk at the time was of saucers and disks.

There are good indications that Rickett knew a great deal

about the Roswell bodies, too. UFO investigator Stan Friedman had the opportunity to speak with Rickett back in the 1980s. It was an absolute cloak-and-dagger-like conversation that was noted not so much for what Rickett *did* say, but for what he *didn't* say. Friedman recalled: "When I mentioned bodies, Rickett clearly reacted and indicated that this was an area he couldn't talk about. He indicated there were different levels of security about this work; that a directive had come down placing this at a high level. He went on to say that certain subjects were discussed only in rooms that couldn't be bugged."

Clearly, Rickett was a concerned man – as he certainly should have been.

* * * * * * * * * * *

A FRIENDLY CALL THAT WASN'T SO FRIENDLY

In other words, decades after the mystifying incident, Rickett was still fearful of saying too much to too many – and particularly so on the matter of the bodies. Nevertheless, it may have been a result of opening his mouth just one too many times that finally led Rickett to get what we might call a friendly warning. You know the sort: they are actually anything *but* friendly. From whom? None other than retired Sheridan Cavitt of the CIC – the man who assured the Air Force in the 1990s that nothing stranger than a weather-balloon was the cause of all the sensational press-coverage way back when, as we'll see later. It was in 1991 when the odd conversation took place. Kevin Randle and Don Schmitt tell the story:

"One can well imagine Bill Rickett's surprise when, after more than 40 years of silence, he received an evening phone call in 1991 from his former commanding officer. 'Happy birthday, Bill,' said the voice on the other end of the phone. 'Its 'Cav,' your old boss.'

"After exchanging niceties, Cavitt queried, 'Have you been talking to anyone about what happened back in 1947?' Rickett identified one investigator, whom Cavitt knew as well.

"'What have you been telling him?' pried Cavitt. 'We both know what really happened out there, don't we, Bill?'

"'We sure do,' Rickett responded.

"After a short pause Cavitt snapped back, 'Well, maybe someday. Goodbye, Bill.'

"Lewis 'Bill' Rickett, who passed away in October 1993, never heard from Cavitt again."

* * * * * * * * * * *

"JAPANESE PLANS TO SEND DISEASE GERMS INTO AMERICA BY BALLOON"

One particularly important fact that many Roswell researchers have either not realized or have carefully avoided highlighting, in case – shock, horror – it dares to support my conclusions, is Dr. Lincoln LaPaz's connection to the issue of Japan's Fugo balloons. In 1945, the University of New Mexico issued a press-release titled "New Mexican Had Lookout Job For 'Japanese Germs.'" It revealed a certain, previously secret, aspect of LaPaz's life, and it reads as follows:

> "Dr. Lincoln LaPaz of the University of New Mexico was in the thick of the fight against Japanese plans to send disease germs into America by balloon, said President J.P Wernette of the University today. Commenting on stories from the Navy in Washington revealing that use of germs and viruses in the Jap balloon-barrage was an enemy project as the war came to an end, Dr. Wernette said that Dr. LaPaz, head of the department of mathematics and the University's Institute of Meteoritics, was with the government's secret anti-balloon project during the war."

University staff continued:

> "'If the war had not ended when it did, in the opening stages of a full-scale balloon offensive which probably would have taken place between October 1945, and now, when the velocity of the west wind at high altitude is greatest, this country would have had unpleasant experiences,' Dr. LaPaz said today. 'People most concerned were trained scientists, and stockmen, too, he said. Anthrax spores could have been sent over in the paper balloons in great numbers, and Manchurian sheep pox could have easily struck the hooved animals of this country because the disease has not been found here and there would be no natural immunity, Dr. LaPaz went on."

LaPaz was quoted as saying: "But the Japanese, using radio devices to locate their balloons on the flight to this country, apparently did not realize that we could pick up the signals an find the balloons before they reached the mainland."

* * * * * * * * * * *

"LAPAZ WAS BUSY IN SECRET GOVERNMENT WORK OF STUDYING AND COMBATING THE BALLOON OFFENSIVE"

A similar press release issued by the University of New Mexico – also in 1945 – details further information on LaPaz's Fugo-themed work for the U.S. military:

> "Observers, watching for meteors, thought they had something when they saw some brilliant lights in the sky from February to May, 1945. And they did, said Dr. Lincoln LaPaz, mathematics department head at the University of New Mexico and director of its Institute of Meteoritics, today. The displays were actually made by Japanese balloons, Dr. LaPaz said, revealing the history of a scientific study of meteors which went on before and during the time that Dr. LaPaz was busy in secret government work of studying and combating the balloon offensive.
>
> "Nevertheless, a few months later, on Nov. 29, 1945, a great meteorite fell slowly across northern California and Nevada, and observers mistook it for everything from a jet plane to a Hollywood publicity stunt. Members of the Society for Research on Meteorites and the American Meteor Society, thought at first that it was a new type [of] Japanese balloon bomb."

If, as the interviewees in my *Body Snatchers in the Desert* book asserted, the key event that led to the legend of the UFO crash at Roswell involved a "next-generation of Fugo" balloon that was responsible for launching an experimental aircraft that catastrophically crashed, then who better to enlist into the study of how and why the experiment failed than an expert on those very same balloons? Namely, Dr. Lincoln LaPaz.

* * * * * * * * * * *

ANOTHER BALLOON, AND NOT A UFO IN SIGHT

There is yet another famous case that has for many years been perceived as a ufological classic, but which also falls under the "secret balloon" category. It occurred just half a year after Roswell. It's the strange and ultimately tragic affair of Kentucky Air National Guard pilot Captain Thomas P. Mantell, who, many UFO believers accept, lost his life chasing a UFO on the afternoon of January 7, 1948. He did not: Mantell died chasing a balloon.

Matters began when personnel at Godman Army Air Field, Kentucky, caught sight of something in the sky they perceived as very strange: a large and extremely reflective object that appeared to be circular in design. No-one could identify it. It was, then, hardly surprising that talk of flying saucers was quickly all-encompassing.

Fortunately, or so it seemed at the time, a squadron of four P51 *Mustang* aircraft was heading towards Godman Army Airfield – a squadron under the command of Captain Mantell. One of the pilots was low on fuel, another one expressed concerns about pursuing the object due to his lack of an oxygen-mask, and a third was ordered to shadow to the ground the pilot who had worries about losing consciousness due to oxygen deprivation. That just left Captain Mantell to pursue the object.

At a height of around 15,000 feet, Mantell called into the base and said that he could see the "UFO" quite clearly. He pushed his plane further through the skies, ultimately reaching a height of approximately 25,000 feet. Then nothing. Apart, that is, from death for the captain, having reached such an altitude without oxygen, Mantell passed out and his plane plummeted to the ground. For many in UFOlogy, the case is a UFO classic. No, it's not. It's a classic *mistake.*

* * * * * * * * * * *

PROTECTING PROJECT SKYHOOK

Unbeknownst to many within the military, at the time of Mantell's encounter, the U.S. Navy's Office of Naval Research had developed, and deployed, massive balloons into the skies of the United States. It was all part of a program called Project Skyhook. For the most part, the balloons captured meteorological data. That did not take away the fact, however, that the existence of the balloons was a well-kept secret. These monster-sized balloons were highly reflective, just as was the object that Mantell encountered. On the subject of Mantell, it's very important to note that he did not have a need-to-know clearance about the work of Project Skyhook.

Staff at the Air Force's UFO program, Project Sign, *were* told of Skyhook, however. This was something which placed Project Sign staff in a very awkward position. They had no desire to tell the world that Mantell had possibly been blown out of the skies by aliens, particularly so because he wasn't. But, due to the highly classified nature of Project Skyhook, they could hardly reveal the truth without also compromising the Navy's project. So, Sign staff offered unlikely suggestions that didn't really convince anyone, such as that perhaps Mantell, in a confused and low-on-oxygen state, was mistakenly chasing the planet Venus. UFO researchers, history has shown, suspected that the military was engaged in a cover-up. Well, yes, it was. But, they weren't hiding a UFO. They were hiding a highly classified balloon.

I bring the Mantell case to your attention for one particular reason. Not because it has a link to Roswell, but because it demonstrates that in terms of national security and secret military programs, in the early years of the Cold War massive balloons, flying saucers, and UFOs very often crossed paths in odd ways that many might think almost unimaginable. In the Roswell case, the truth was hidden behind a barrier of tales of UFOs, weather-balloons and Project Mogul balloons. In the Mantell case, the military couldn't reveal what they really knew, because doing so would have opened up a large can of worms about the balloon-based Project Skyhook.

Indeed, and as Dr. David Clarke – the author of, among others, *How UFOs Conquered the World* – noted in 2015, with regard to Project Skyhook and Mantell: "In 2004 a former member of the project's staff, Duke Gildenberg, revealed the Office of Naval Research had monitored press reports of flying saucer sightings to track the movements of their balloons. The Mantell incident was an early indication of the problems – and solutions – that mass belief in UFOs could provide for intelligence agencies."

* * * * * * * * * * *

"THE ONLY AUTHENTIC JAPANESE FLYING SAUCER EVER RECOVERED IN THIS COUNTRY"

A very curious UFO-themed story surfaced in May 1949. It caught the attention of the FBI, which had been keeping a careful watch on the subject since the summer of 1947, when the flying saucer exploded on the world stage, as we have seen. On May 26, an FBI document – captioned "Flying Discs" – was written and revealed the facts concerning a strange saga. It stated: "Walter Winchell forwarded to the Director a Western Union telegram he had received from Robert Ripley [of "Ripley's Believe It Or Not!"] which stated that he, Ripley, had the only authentic Japanese flying saucer ever recovered in this country. Mr. Winchell noted on the telegram, 'To J. Edgar Hoover – True?'

> "This matter was discussed with Colonel [deleted], OSI-USAF, who advised on April 27, 1949 that he had interested himself in the flying saucers and related subjects and that in so far as could be determined by him through his sources in the Air Force, which are excellent, there is no authentic information available concerning the phenomenon of flying saucers. He advised he would check with the authorities at Wright Field to determine if any information is available concerning the recovery of a Japanese flying saucer.
>
> "Colonel [deleted] has now advised that there is no information available in any arm of the Air Force to the effect that any flying saucers of any kind have

been recovered in the United States. Colonel [deleted] stated delay had been encountered in determining this fact inasmuch as inquiries had been directed through individuals known to him and trusted by him and not through the usual channels from which he possibly would receive a stock answer."

* * * * * * * * * * *

"FLYING DISK HYSTERIA"

It turned out that this particular Japanese saucer was nothing of the sort. It was a good-natured hoax, mixed with a liberal degree of misidentification and exaggeration. With Robert Ripley involved, how could it have been much else? Rather ironically, however, the Air Force's Office of Special Investigations was still worried. The OSI's concern was that members of the public who might stumble on the remains of Japanese Fugo balloons - which were still being occasionally found across the United States, four years after the war was over – could mistakenly interpret them as flying saucers. And, in a worst case scenario, blow themselves to pieces if the bombs were still in working order. It's most intriguing, therefore, that the OSI suggested it would be very wise to take seriously any and all reports of "debris remains of Japanese balloons which might cause flying disk hysteria."

The FBI drew parallels between Fugo balloons and flying saucers midway through 1947. Dr. Lincoln LaPaz was up to his neck in those same balloons during the Second World War. Roswell fixture, Bill Rickett, hung out with LaPaz in New Mexico as the good doc sought to secretly solve certain aspects of the Roswell crash. And, we know that the Air Force was also making a Fugo-UFO connection in 1949. From the very earliest days of UFOlogy, Japan's balloons and flying saucers were regular bedfellows.

6:

FROM JAPAN TO THE FOSTER RANCH

"BACTERIOLOGICAL Warfare in the United States" is a fascinating FBI document that was declassified into the public domain in 2006, via the terms of the Freedom of Information Act, and covers the years 1941 to 1950. Notably, of the file's original 1,783 pages, no less than 1,074 have been firmly withheld from declassification by the FBI. The file reveals a wealth of illuminating and disturbing data on animal disease and death, and their potential, theoretical links to bacteriological warfare and sabotage by enemy nations and individuals.

In a strange and winding way, the story the file tells has a bearing on the theme of this book. Much of the dossier is focused on a series of mysterious and suspicious outbreaks of disease – and attendant death – in Lincoln County, New Mexico in the 1940s, which is the very same county where the Roswell event occurred. Not only that, as will soon become clear, there is even a Japanese balloon link to the Lincoln County outbreak.

* * * * * * * * * * * *

"THE NEW MEXICO PUBLIC HEALTH AUTHORITY HAS BEEN ON THE ALERT"

In late 1950, the New Mexico State Public Health Laboratory sent a memo to the FBI which read as follows:

> "Possibly some of you saw headlines in newspapers published in the States during August, such as 'Black Death Stirs Albuquerque,' 'Black Plague Hits Two in New Mexico,' and 'Dark Age Plague Found in Two.' It is unfortunate that we must still seriously discuss plague, for we already know so much about its cause and mode of spread; but as long as such headlines do occur, it is necessary that we who are interested in Public Health and Preventive Medicine do seriously consider plague and acquaint ourselves with the plague of today, its prevalence, and its potentialities."

The FBI was particularly worried about the New Mexico outbreaks and recorded the following:

> "The New Mexico Public Health Authority has been on the alert for cases of plague since 1938 when the U.S. Public Health Service first reported plague in the wild rodents of one of our counties. There was no suggestion of human infection until August 1, 1949, when the Laboratory received a request for aid in the diagnosis of two cases. A slide made from material aspirated from an axillary bubo [swelling of the lymph nodes] of a ten-year-old boy of Taos County was first received.
>
> "Late on August 1, 1949, the pathologist at the Veteran's Hospital in Albuquerque called stating that a man from Placitas, Sandoval County, had been admitted to the hospital and his clinical symptoms resembled plague. The cases were from areas 200 miles apart with no connection. The little boy of Taos probably received

his infection from a bit of a flea escaped from the body of a prairie dog which he killed by throwing a stone. The man from Sandoval probably received his infection from fleas from ground squirrels that he had killed while working on his farm.

"These two New Mexico cases of human plague are good examples of what might be expected considering the reservoir of plague infection in the wild rodents of the western states.Very possibly there are undiagnosed human cases in New Mexico and other states with widely scattered population."

* * * * * * * * * * *

"A CLEAR HISTORY COULD NOT BE OBTAINED"

A further document from this particular collection of formerly classified papers provides this:

"Since this report was written, a 7 ½ year-old-boy in Lincoln County died, possibly of plague. The boy was taken to a physician at Fort Stanton, November 4. Apparently he was not in a very serious condition and was sent home. He was returned to the Fort Stanton Hospital November 5 in the morning; his temperature was somewhat higher; by noon he was markedly worse, and by 2:30 he was dead. A post mortem examination was made and the doctor in charge diagnosed the case as being bubonic plague with pneumonic and septicemic complications. Portions of the organs were sent to [name deleted] at the

> Western Communicable Disease Laboratory in San Francisco; and he confirmed the child was probably infected by ectoparasites from tree squirrels. A clear history could not be obtained, but dead tree squirrels were found in the barn and near the dwelling of this child."

As a result of all this disturbing activity, the FBI turned its attention towards securing as many newspaper articles as possible that had been published on the subject of plague and other, potentially fatal, conditions in New Mexico. There was, for example, "Lea Rabbits Suspected Bubonic Plague Carriers," which appeared in the pages of the *Albuquerque Journal* on June 21, 1950. Now, we come to an even more eye-opening series of revelations on this issue.

* * * * * * * * * * *

A JAPANESE BALLOON IN LINCOLN COUNTY?

So concerned was the FBI by these various outbreaks of plague in New Mexico in 1949, J. Edgar Hoover took secret steps to share all of the pertinent medical data – and media articles, too – with a fistful of agencies of the government and the military. They included the U.S. Air Force's Director of Special Investigations, the Director of Naval Intelligence, the Acting Director of the Division of Security of the Atomic Energy Commission, and the Director of the CIA. The most important point of all will now be revealed. It demonstrates precisely why a wide and varied body of intelligence agencies were carefully, and secretly, monitoring this situation.

Additional files on this issue surfaced after the FBI's release of material in 2006; this time, from the Air Force Office of Special

Investigations. There was a school of thought within certain factions of the AFOSI that while the plague deaths very likely resulted from flea bites and attacks by infected animals, the plague itself may have been *deliberately* released in Lincoln County, New Mexico, by nothing less than...*a Japanese balloon*. Probably in 1945, it was surmised – which is when the Fugo raids were at their height. The theory was that due to the small, isolated, human populations in some of the areas where plague broke out, it may have taken several years before the plague took hold in the animal population and then jumped to people.

The shared, secret files also reveal that some authorities believed – years later and with the benefit of hindsight – that the initial outbreak in Lincoln County was caused by the Hantavirus, which was first acknowledged by the West in the early 1950s and at the height of the Korean War.

Of greatest importance, however, is a document titled "Japanese Balloon Raids – 1945" which was found in the archives of what, in the 1940s, was called Camp Detrick. Today, it goes by the name of Fort Detrick. Located in Maryland, the facility is at the forefront of research into bacteriological warfare, chemical warfare, and lethal viruses. The document postulates that in 1945 a Japanese Fugo balloon came down somewhere in Lincoln County and unleashed a deadly cargo of plague-infected insects – such as fleas – and which eventually took hold, leading to the unfortunate death of the young boy at Fort Stanton, four years later.

Then, there is this from Fort Stanton's website: "Fort Stanton became America's first federal tuberculosis hospital and first German internment camp during World War II. The Fort also served as home to Japanese interned during the war, and State prisoners recovering from substance abuse."

Also on the matter of Fort Stanton, we will later learn a great deal more about this intrigue-filled installation and its ties to the July 1947 crash, to a surviving crew-member of the ill-fated flight that caused all of the fuss, to unusual-looking people, and to the startling findings of a UFO investigator and conspiracy-theorist, the late Kathy Kasten, who died in 2012.

* * * * * * * * * * *

RAINING DOWN ON ROSWELL AND THE RANCH

This strange story contains all of the threads that my sources said became part of the Roswell legend: (a) Japanese balloons, (b) a military installation housing state prisoners, and (c) Japanese people. And, let's not forget, it all took place in Lincoln County – the home of the controversial "UFO crash."

The Roswell story is clearly *way more* complex than many have assumed – and it was infinitely complex from the very beginning! We may well have seen two things occur in Lincoln County: (a) the landing of a Fugo balloon in 1945 that let loose something dangerous, deadly and bacteriological and which took significant hold in the immediate years ahead, and (b) the crash of a vehicle two years later, in 1947, on the Foster Ranch – an event which *also* had a Japanese / balloon component attached to it.

Now, some might find that too incredible, and too coincidental, to accept. But, it should be noted that, by Mack Brazel's very own admission, prior to the events of July 1947, he had found balloons on the ranch on no less than *two previous occasions*. Not toy balloons, I should stress, but military weather balloons. Brazel told the press he was sure the latest, and most notorious, find of all was not a weather balloon. But, with the military running the show, he was forced to stay tight-lipped on what he really knew about the craft and the bodies. Brazel was right about it not being a weather balloon. It was altogether a different kind of balloon – or, rather, an entire array of them.

A good, solid case can be made that the whole area was *teeming* with things of a military nature in the 1940s; things that fell out of the sky back then on more than a few occasions, many of them of a balloon-based nature. Sue Farnsworth, for example, has spoken about how her father, Arthur Farnsworth, who owned Roswell Auto Co., was threatened by the military in 1947 over what went on "out there" at the ranch. Interestingly, the Farnsworth family had its very own ranch, located northwest of Roswell. Sue Farnsworth noted something that I find to be most significant: "We were used to finding 'funny things' from White Sands on our ranch all the time, but this was clearly something different judging by the military reaction."

The reaction may well have been markedly different, but that still allows for the craft that came down to have originated at White Sands, rather than in the depths of outer space. What this all means is that the events which became known as "the Roswell Incident" were so controversial that they had to be hidden – and at all costs. Lincoln County and the Roswell area, it seems, were *swarming* with classified balloon-linked / -based programs in the latter years of the 1940s. And the creations of those programs were raining down on the good folk of New Mexico on a regular basis. No wonder it was so easy to hide one highly controversial balloon-based program with another of a far less inflammatory and weather-based nature.

7:

WHEN THE SUNSHINE TURNED DARK

AS the 1940s gave way to a new decade, controversial research undertaken on human beings continued. Not for medical reasons, but for purposes that were of benefit to the military. And it continued undercover of a massive amount of secrecy and security. There were very good reasons for that, as we shall see. One of the things I heard time and again when my *Body Snatchers in the Desert* book was published in the summer of 2005, was that not only was there no evidence to support the notion that diabolical human-experimentation was the cause of the Roswell controversy; but, in addition, there was no way that government and military agencies, offices and departments would ever even consider engaging in - or sanction - such terrible actions. Really? I have to say that the faith and trust (or, as I prefer to call it, the outright, naive gullibility) that people have in government never ceases to amaze me.

For what is perhaps the most shocking example of the way in which human beings were indeed utilized for radiation-related experiments at the height of the Cold War, we have to turn our attention to something called Project Sunshine. There was nothing bright and sunny about this program, however.

Although not directly allied with the events as described in my book, the history and activities of Project Sunshine collectively serve as perfect examples (and perhaps far more importantly as *officially documented* examples) of the way in which human beings and bodies were utilized in Cold War radiation and biological experimentation in a fashion very similar to the top secret Roswell-related events as detailed in *Body Snatchers in the Desert.*

In the 1990s, the Government's Advisory Committee on Human Radiation Experiments looked into a whole range of Department of Energy-related scandals involving the use of human beings in radiation tests from the 1940s to the 1970s. What the committee found shocked and outraged them.

* * * * * * * * * * *

BODY-SNATCHING CONTINUES - INTO THE FIFTIES

One particular memorandum, dated June 9, 1995, and prepared by ACHRE's Advisory Committee Staff, is titled *Documentary Update on Project Sunshine Body Snatching* and states:

> "As part of Project Sunshine, which sought to measure strontium-90, the AEC [Atomic Energy Commission] engaged in an effort to collect baby bones from domestic and foreign sources. As discussed in the prior memorandum, the project involved the use of a cover story (those without clearance being told that the skeleton collection would be used to study naturally occurring radiation, and not that from fallout). Key participants in Project Sunshine at its onset included the AEC's Division of Biology and Medicine (DBM), its Director John Bugher, Columbia University's Dr. J. Laurence Kulp, and the University of Chicago's Dr. Willard Libby (who became an AEC Commissioner)."

The memorandum then refers to Dr. Willard Libby and his work in more detail. A 1955 transcript classified as "Secret" (located in the classified materials at the National Archives and declassified at the Committee's request), sheds more light on the role of tissue sampling in Project Sunshine. The transcript shows that, from the early to mid-1950s, considerable thought had been devoted to best ways to establish channels to procure "human samples," and the impact of secrecy on the effort. AEC Commissioner Willard Libby, who was a primary proponent of Project Sunshine, explained the great value of "body snatching," and noted that the AEC had even employed an "expensive law firm" to "look up the law of body snatching."

* * * * * * * * * * *

"IF ANYBODY KNOWS HOW TO DO A GOOD JOB OF BODY SNATCHING, THEY WILL REALLY BE SERVING THEIR COUNTRY"

The meeting was then turned over to Dr. Libby, who was by now an AEC Commissioner. Dr. Libby began by stating that there was no effort more important to the AEC than Sunshine. However, he said that "...there are great gaps in the data." He elaborated: "By far the most important [gap] is human samples. We have been reduced to essentially zero level on the human samples. I don't know how to get them but I do say that it is a matter of prime importance to get them and particularly in the young age group."

The supply of stillborns had evidently been shut off: ""We were fortunate, as you know to obtain a large number of stillborns as material. This supply, however, has now been cut off also, and shows no signs, I think, of being rejuvenated."

Therefore, Libby told the audience, expertise in body snatching would be highly valued: "So human samples are of prime importance and if anybody knows how to do a good job of body snatching, they will really be serving their country."

Some people reading this, no doubt, will scarcely believe that these latter words were said in all seriousness, and soberly recorded, within official files of the U.S. military. As noted, Libby recalled that when Project Sunshine was created in 1953, a law firm was hired to study this problem. He added: "I don't know how to snatch bodies. In the original study on the Sunshine at Rand in the summer of 1953, we hired an expensive law firm to look up the law of body snatching. This compendium is available to you. It is not very encouraging. It shows you how very difficult it is going to be to do legally."

The conference attendees discussed the need for a wide enough variety of samples to cover age ranges and potential variations among body parts. A Dr. Kulp, from Columbia, explained that there were certain "channels" available:

> "We have the channels in these places where we are getting everything. We have three or four other leads where we could get complete age range samples from different other geographic localities. These three are Vancouver, Houston, and New York. We could easily get them from Puerto Rico and other places. We can get virtually everyone that dies in this range."

All of the haziness in the paragraph directly above smacks of acquiring "samples" via not-exactly-legal routes.

* * * * * * * * * * *

"SPECIMENS" AND "RESOURCES"

There was also discussion of the need to acquire what were insultingly termed as "resources" from other countries. For example, a Colonel Maxwell, of the Armed Forces Special Weapons Project, suggested the military could provide some help in securing "specimens" from a native hospital in Formosa. In case you're wondering, or you haven't deduced, in the files the terms "resources" and "specimens" refer to people.

This passage is particularly revealing for one reason: when I was doing the research for my *Body Snatchers in the Desert* book, I was told by several sources that personnel from the Armed Forces Special Weapons Project were deeply involved in the recovery of alleged handicapped Japanese bodies from a 1947 incident at White Sands, New Mexico – not Roswell, but another incident that ended very badly. It is, therefore, notable that in 1955, when the Project Sunshine discussions were well underway, one Colonel Maxwell, also of the Armed Forces Special Weapons Project, stated firmly that he knew how to acquire certain 'specimen' from 'a native hospital in Formosa…'

Interestingly, when this testimony became public knowledge, new sources surfaced with their own dark and disturbing tales. They centered upon radiation experiments involving the bodies of children and physically handicapped and deformed individuals. Reuters, for example, ran an article on June 6, 2001 titled "Babies and Stillborns Used in Nuclear Experiments." It included the following, stark words:

> "British newspapers reported that some 6,000 stillborn babies and dead infants were sent from hospitals in Australia, Canada, Hong Kong, South America, the UK and the US between the 1950s and 1970s without the permission of parents for use in nuclear experiments. According to the reports, the US Department of Energy used the bodies and some body parts for tests to monitor radioactivity levels of the element Strontium 90 in humans...The Observer, a British newspaper, also stated that British scientists also conducted tests on babies sent from Hong Kong and the research did not end until the 1970s. A government spokesman for Hong Kong announced that his country will investigate further into the reports."

* * * * * * * * * * *

"WE DIDN'T FLY THEM OUT AGAIN"

On June 12, 2001 – which was less than a week after Reuters unveiled its shocking story, Western Australia Newspapers Ltd., (WAN) published that: "...people with severe disabilities were used as human guinea pigs during British nuclear tests at the Maralinga Test Site in Australia in the 1950s."

For those who aren't aware of the history of all this, take note of the words of the BBC's Sydney, Australia correspondent, Jon Donnison:

> "It seems remarkable today but less than 60 years ago, Britain was exploding nuclear bombs in the middle of

> Australia. In the mid-1950s, seven bombs were tested at Maralinga in the south-west Australian outback. The combined force of the weapons doubled that of the bomb dropped on the Japanese city of Hiroshima in World War Two.
>
> "In archive video footage, British and Australian soldiers can be seen looking on, wearing short sleeves and shorts and doing little to protect themselves other than turning their backs and covering their eyes with their hands. Some reported the flashes of the blasts being so bright that they could see the bones of their fingers, like x-rays, as they pressed against their faces."

According to the information highlighted by Western Australia Newspapers Ltd., however, there was far more to the affair than that. According to the allegations, a control group was flown to the British test site as part of an experiment to determine the effects of radiation on humans. The group, stated the WAN, died after being exposed to the radioactive fallout. While such claims were dismissed as unsubstantiated in a final report of a royal commission into British nuclear tests in Australia in December 1985, no less a source than Dr. Robert Jackson, Director of the Center for Disability Research and Development at Edith Cowan University in Australia, expressed concern that the Royal Commission did not hear testimonials from pilots.

Dr. Jackson discovered details of these gruesome events in the 1980s, when he was the Regional Director for the Western Australia Disability Commission. Of key relevance to the subject matter of this book, is an approach made to Dr. Jackson by a man who claimed to be a pilot and who had flown a "planeload" of disabled, physically handicapped people from the U.K. to the Maralinga Test Site. The pilot told Dr. Jackson, "We didn't fly them out again."

Needless to say, I don't find this last statement at all surprising - unfortunately.

8:

"THE PLANNED USE OF PROPAGANDA"

ACCORDING to a Technical Report prepared by the Air Force's UFO study-program, Project Grudge, way back in August of 1949: "Upon eliminating several additional incidents due to vagueness and duplication, there remain 228 incidents, which are considered in this report. Thirty of these could not be explained, because there was found to be insufficient evidence on which to base a conclusion."

Certainly the most notable entry in the document appears in the "Recommendations" section. It states, and I quote: "...that Psychological Warfare Division and other governmental agencies interested in psychological warfare be informed of the results of this study."

The U.S. Department of Defense defines PW as: "The planned use of propaganda and other psychological actions having the primary purpose of influencing the opinions, emotions, attitudes, and behavior of hostile foreign groups in such a way as to support the achievement of national objectives."

What this demonstrates, is that the military's UFO programs weren't just about investigating sightings. The operations were also focused on creating utterly bogus flying saucer-themed stories – all born out of psychological warfare operations designed to hide things of a *non*-UFO nature. Which is exactly what happened at Roswell – a spurious tale of a saucer was spun to hide something that the government wanted hidden. And it *was* hidden.

* * * * * * * * * * *

"WAS THIS ACTUALLY NOTHING TO DO WITH REAL SAUCERS BUT INSTEAD SOME SORT OF PSYCHOLOGICAL WARFARE OPERATION?"

The late Karl Pflock and "a highly secret U.S. Government entity" (Nick Redfern)

There is also the matter of the infamous, alleged UFO crash at Aztec, New Mexico in March 1948. It's a story which is made famous in Frank Scully's 1950 book, *Behind the Flying Saucers*, a book which turned out to be a huge seller. Many researchers of the UFO phenomenon (although certainly not all, such as Scott and Suzanne Ramsey,) dismiss Aztec as nothing but a hoax, one perpetrated by a shady businessman/conman named Silas Newton.

There is an interesting aspect to the Newton / Aztec story which is worth noting. By his own admittance, and after the

Aztec story surfaced, Newton was clandestinely visited by two representatives of "a highly secret U.S. Government entity," as the late Karl Pflock worded it. Those same representatives told Newton, in no uncertain terms, that they knew his Aztec story was a complete and bald-faced lie. Incredibly, though, they wanted him to keep telling the tale to just about anyone and everyone who would listen.

This led Pflock to wonder: "Did the U.S. Government or someone associated with it use Newton to discredit the idea of crashed flying saucers so a real captured saucer or saucers could be more easily kept under wraps?"

Far more intriguing, though, is the next question that Karl posed: "Was this actually nothing to do with real saucers but instead *some sort of psychological warfare operation* [italics mine]?"

Pflock - a CIA intelligence officer, and a Deputy Assistant Secretary of Defense in the Reagan Administration - was not just fascinated by the Aztec saga of 1948, per se. He was also fascinated by the possibility that someone in the government, the intelligence community, or the military – and maybe even a combination of all three – had created the story to hide something else. Or, at the very least, had *encouraged* the telling and retelling of the Aztec story for psy-op-based reasons.

* * * * * * * * * * *

"SILAS THE MAGNIFICENT"

I know just how fascinated Karl was when it came to Aztec and the claims of Newton and that "highly secret U.S. Government entity." I first met Karl in 2003 – at a UFO gig in the small town of Aztec, New Mexico. For a number of years, the conference was a yearly event. But, no more. Karl and I were were in touch by landline and fax (how quaint) as far back as the mid-1990s. When Karl and I finally met, he near-immediately suggested that we should write an Aztec-themed book. Karl's reasoning was that he knew the story very well, and, via the provisions of the Freedom of Information Act, I had uncovered hundreds and hundreds of pages of material – chiefly from the FBI – on the Aztec controversy. He thought we would make a good team, and particularly so now that I lived in the U.S. – and in Texas, which is, of course, not at all far from New Mexico, where Karl resided and where the 1948 crash supposedly happened.

As I listened, Karl told me that his idea was, essentially, to make the book a biography on Newton, but with the Aztec affair being the main thrust. I thought it was a good idea and Karl suggested he prepare a synopsis for his literary agent, Cherry Weiner. Which is exactly what he did. The book was going to be called *Silas the Magnificent: A True Tale of Greed, Credulity, and (Maybe) Government Chicanery and Cover-up in 1950s America.* Note that the book makes no mention of UFOs in its title and sub-title.

Unfortunately, the project was permanently derailed when Karl fell sick with Amyotrophic Lateral Sclerosis, also referred to as Lou Gehrig's disease. He unfortunately died from the effects of ALS on June 5, 2006, at the age of sixty-three. Karl is gone, but the synopsis still exists. It would have made a good book. And, very possibly, it just might have revealed more of the psy-op aspect of Aztec and of other crashed UFO yarns of bygone decades.

* * * * * * * * * * *

FROM ROSWELL TO "RADIATION EXPERIMENTS"

It's also very worth noting that Karl Pflock was – initially, at least - extremely vocal on the issue of whether or not some form of secret terrestrial device came to grief at Roswell. Commenting in 1994 on the allegations that alien bodies were recovered in the New Mexico area as part of the so-called Roswell incident, Pflock was willing, at the time, to conclude that there were indeed "human-like but strangely disfigured bodies" recovered in the New Mexico desert in 1947; and that those same bodies were "associated with some very unusual wreckage."

Pflock was careful to point out that: "Even if there were bodies - and I believe there were - they may not have been of unearthly origin. In which case, Roswell turns out to be a significant chapter in early Cold War history, akin to the currently unfolding disclosures about the U.S. government radiation experiments spawned in the same era."

It's very important to note that Karl later changed his opinion, quite radically, and became a champion of the theory that what was recovered at Roswell was nothing more extraordinary than a Mogul balloon. Yet, it is interesting that his initial thoughts veered towards the possibility of an event connected to "U.S. government radiation experiments."

Moving on from Aztec…

* * * * * * * * * * * *

A CRASHED UFO "PLANT"

For many years, rumors have circulated to the effect that in the early 1950s a UFO crashed on the island of Spitsbergen, Norway. And, that under circumstances similar to those that allegedly occurred at Aztec, New Mexico, in 1948, the unearthly craft was recovered, along with its deceased, alien crew. It transpires that a reference to this case can be found in a UFO-themed document that surfaced under the terms of the U.S. Freedom of Information Act from the National Security Agency.

The NSA's copy is slightly different to copies of the same document that have been declassified by the Air Force, the Department of State, and the Army. Someone in the NSA – unfortunately, we don't know who – identified the Spitsbergen story in the document as a "plant." As to who secretly seeded the story and why, that's another matter entirely, one that is probably now lost to the fog of time.

Now, it's time to turn our attention to the next decade, the 1960s – a period which brought another revelation of the Roswell variety.

9:

"THEY COULD HAVE PASSED FOR CHINESE"

IT is well worth noting that in the early 1960s an event occurred in the wilds of Scotland which eerily paralleled the Roswell affair of 1947. Yes, we are talking about a clandestine balloon flight that was given a spaceship-driven spin. In a July 2012 article at his blog titled "The Scottish Roswell?" Dr. David Clarke said of this curious case:

> "Picture the scene: A shepherd visiting a remote area stumbles upon strange wreckage strewn across the ground which could be the remains of a crashed spaceship. The debris consists of pieces of unusual metal and strange drawings. Once the find is reported at the local police station, search teams and military personnel descend on the area. The wreckage disappears – no one knows where – and civilians are told to 'keep quiet about it.'
>
> "You are probably thinking 'Roswell, New Mexico, 1947.'
>
> "But no, this incident occurred in the Scottish Highlands one spring morning in 1962. It has uncanny links to its American cousin, even down to the 'cover story' used hide the true identity and purpose of the 'crashed spaceship.'"

The case to which Dr. Clarke refers occurred on the wild moorland in Ardgay, Scotland. In the same way that rancher Brazel reported his find to the authorities in 1947, a shepherd named Donald MacKenzie did likewise: he contacted the local police and told them what he had found. A four-man Royal Air Force team – attached to the RAF Mountain Rescue Service - traveled to the area and found both the site and the odd materials. Attempts on the part of Squadron Leader John Sims, of Royal Air Force Kinloss, to learn what had come down, failed: he was told by the Air Ministry, London, that it was absolutely none of his business. Data that appeared in base logbooks was confiscated. The mystery was quickly and effectively hidden. The only thing missing from this saga was a bunch of dead aliens strewn across the moors of Ardgay. Nevertheless, it's still a story that contains all the key ingredients of a ufological pot-boiler!

Except for one thing: At its heart was something very different to a UFO. Dr. Clarke decided to dig deep into the story. He did more than that: he solved the decades-old mystery. The wreckage found at Ardgay was not from a crashed flying saucer. It was, in reality, debris from a huge balloon attached to a CIA-funded, classified program called Moby Dick.

Air Vectors notes: "The first Moby Dick launch was on 19 February 1953. 640 Moby Dick balloons were launched up to the end of the program on 30 June 1954. For whatever reasons, a range of different balloon configurations were used during the program, with balloon diameters ranging from 15 meters (49 feet) to 25 meters (83 feet), and shapes including cylinders."

The similarities between the Scottish event of 1962 and that which occurred at Roswell in 1947 are as clear as they are obvious. Yet again, we see the development of a mystery with clear

UFO-themed overtones attached to it, but which actually had very down to earth – but highly secret – balloon-based origins. Maybe Roswell and Ardgay should become twin-towns.

* * * * * * * * * * *

ROSWELL AND FRANK EDWARDS

Although research into the Roswell affair didn't take off big time until the mid-to-late 1970s, the 1960s were not without significance when it comes to the case. In 1966, Frank Edwards' book *Flying Saucers – Serious Business* was published. Chapter four – Pick Up the Pieces, Edwards said of the case:

> "There are such difficult cases as the rancher near Roswell, New Mexico, who phoned the Sheriff that a blazing disc-shaped object had passed over his house at low altitude and had crashed and burned on a hillside within view of the house. The sheriff called the military; the military came on the double quick. Newsmen were not permitted in the area. A week later, however, the government released a photograph of a service man holding up a box kite with an aluminum disc about the size of a large pie plate dangling from the bottom of the kite. This, the official report explained, was a device borne aloft on the kite and used to test radar gear by bouncing the signals off the pie pan. And this, we were told, was the sort of thing that had so excited the rancher. We were NOT told, however, how the alleged kite caught fire – nor why the military cordoned off the area while

> they inspected the wreckage of a burned-out kite with a non-inflammable pie pan tied to it."

Kevin Randle said of Edwards' version of events: "While the report was essentially correct in a gross sense, the details were nearly all wrong. But the point is that Edwards had exposed the Roswell case to a wide audience in 1966, when the book was published. Nearly everyone ignored the case because of the lack of detail, other than a location in the then small and anonymous town of Roswell."

Only three years later, however, the Roswell story was about to surface again. Not in the pages of a book, or even in the town of Roswell itself. The location was one most would never guess: a certain living-room in England.

* * * * * * * * * * *

A FAMILY LEARNS A BIG SECRET

July 21, 1969 was a day on which history was made. That was the date on which Neil Armstrong became the very first member of the human race to set foot on our nearest neighbor, the Moon. History was also made in a very different way on that day, too. It may have been different, but it was no less important. For the person telling the story, it may have been even *more* important. July 21 was the day on which a notable revelation concerning Roswell surfaced. Not in the United States, as one might expect or assume, but right in the heart of the U.K.

The source of the story was Melvin E. Brown, a man who was stationed at the Roswell Army Air Field at the time of the mysterious crash in early July 1947. Several months later, however, Brown was given a brand new assignment. In England. It was while Brown was stationed in the United Kingdom that he met the woman who was destined to become his wife Ada. The pair made a life for themselves in England and had three daughters. At the time of the Roswell affair, however, Brown was a sergeant in the military. Not only that, Brown – who passed away in 1986 – was a key figure in the Roswell story.

Whether by accident or design, Brown chose July 21 as the day to reveal what he knew about a certain amazing event that had occurred, back then, more than two decades earlier. One of Brown's daughters – Beverly – said, years later: "In 1969, he told my sister and me that he was ordered to go out into the desert. He said that all available men were grabbed to go out to where a crashed saucer had come down…and there were several bodies."

Roswell: "UFO Central" (Nick Redfern)

* * * * * * * * * * *

"BIG HEADS WITH SLANTED EYES"

One of those who had the opportunity to interview Beverly in person was English UFO sleuth, Timothy Good, the author of the acclaimed *Above Top Secret*. She told him: "They had to form a ring around whatever it was they had to cover, and everything was put on trucks. They were told not to look and to take no notice, and were sworn to secrecy."

The story then got even more amazing, as Beverley revealed: "I can remember my dad saying he couldn't understand why they wanted refrigerated trucks. And him and another guy had to sit on the back of a truck to take this stuff to a hangar. They were packed in ice. And he lifted up the tarpaulin and looked in, and saw three – or possibly two – dead bodies."

Tom Carey and Don Schmitt record that Beverly described the dead crew as having "big heads with slanted eyes." In her interview with Tim Good, however, Beverly made a very intriguing and revealing statement. She said that the bodies her father saw back in '47 "...*looked Asian* [italics mine]," but had larger than normal heads and lacked any hair. "They looked a yellowy color." There is also this from Beverly to Tim: "...*they could have passed for Chinese* [italics also mine]."

It is one thing to say that the bodies looked somewhat Asian; however, stating that the bodies which Melvin Brown saw "could have passed for Chinese" strongly suggests they were *extremely* human-looking. There is a very good reason for that: they *were* human. Remember too that the "Chinese" comment was made to Beverly Bean by her father – a first-hand witness to the bodies. And, as a first-hander he should have known what it was that he saw.

Near death in 1986, Brown told his family, "It was not a damn weather balloon."

No, it was not.

* * * * * * * * * * *

"I ALMOST CHOKED ON MY COFFEE"

Moving into the 1970s and the 1980s, we have three very intriguing stories from John A. Price of the Roswell-based UFO Enigma Museum and the author of a 1997 non-fiction book, *Roswell: A Quest for the Truth.* On one particular day in 1978, Price – who was employed as a roofer at the time - was working outside on a particular property in Hagerman. It's a town situated approximately twenty-four miles from Roswell. The property held a number of handicapped children – this much was clear to Price, as several such children exited the property and stood on the patio, watching him as he worked. He thought "this must be a home for the mentally impaired."

That was not all, however. Price had more to say: "Suddenly, I almost choked on my coffee as two more children, or at least I think they were children, walked out and stood behind the others."

According to Price, they were all around four- to four-and-a-half-feet in height. They had oversized, hairless heads, and their ears and noses were noticeably smaller than normal for a young child. Things came to a sudden end when, Price recalls, "a lady came to the door and ushered the kids back into the house."

He did not see them again.

* * * * * * * * * * *

"THERE WERE SOME PRETTY DEFORMED YOUNG MEN THERE"

More than a decade later, Price received a letter from "an acquaintance" who he had known for some time. Price said, "in the letter he told me that the aliens I was looking for were at Fort Stanton."

For those who may not know, Fort Stanton is a military installation which, during the Second World War, held a number of Japanese "enemy aliens," and which is barely spitting distance away from the Foster Ranch. We will learn *a great deal* more about Fort Stanton's wartime Japanese connections in later chapters – as well as its links to Roswell. In the meantime, back to Price.

Price's source told him that at some undisclosed point, "there were some pretty deformed young men there, several of which could be of alien nature. We only went by what we were told; please don't tell anyone. Mongoloid large heads, small ears, pin heads who could function and had shrill voices. They were supposed to be of incest, but from their looks – Outa-space."

Price took the story seriously, and mused on the possibility that the government may have grabbed handicapped people who had "no paper trail, no social security number, and no traceable family connections."

Nightmarish? No doubt. Right on target? That depends on the extent of your "I want to believe" factor.

Someone else who suspected that Roswell could be explained in down to earth – rather than alien – fashion was yet another acquaintance of Price. His name was Robert Betz, an engineer who, prior to his retirement, had been contracted to various corporations to perform certain sensitive work. Price said, "Robert was convinced that the Roswell crash could be explained away as a top secret project of flying saucer design and that the bodies were midgets."

Now it's time to head off to the 1990s, a decade in which interest in Roswell soared, and commentary and theories for the crash were flying around in wild fashion.

10:

"IT WAS RUMORED THAT THEY WERE HUMAN EXPERIMENTS"

THE late Leonard Stringfield, who passed away in 1994, was a UFO researcher who firmly believed that, since the 1940s, the U.S. Government had secretly recovered a number of crashed UFOs and dead aliens, and which were stored and preserved at a variety of military bases across the country – many at Wright-Patterson Air Force Base, Ohio. Stringfield too, however, was given a number of accounts relative to the issue of secret and shocking human experimentation on handicapped people; experimentation that was tied in with the Roswell affair.

One of those stories came to Stringfield from a highly controversial figure in UFOlogy. His name was Timothy Cooper, a resident of Big Bear Lake, California and someone who exited the field of UFO research years ago. Far more than a few people in UFOlogy have very little time for Cooper, suspecting that many of the documents he supplied to the UFO community in the mid-1990s were bogus, rather than the highly classified papers that they were purported to be. They *were* bogus; there is no doubt about that. But, Cooper himself was not the forger. It's the "pre-documents" era we have to take a look at, however. It paints a very different picture of Cooper to that which many ufologists have accepted.

Tim Cooper claimed to Stringfield in 1990 that he had numerous sources of the old-timer kind – some of who assured

Cooper that, yes, aliens really did crash outside of Roswell in the summer of 1947. Others, however, quietly hinted to Cooper that the truth was far more controversial: a scenario involving human guinea-pigs – Japanese and handicapped individuals - and the creation of UFO-themed disinformation programs and faked pro-UFO documents to hide the down-to-earth truth of the Roswell enigma.

Also in 1990, Cooper supplied Stringfield one story which Stringfield decided to firmly keep under wraps until the following year, 1991, when he published it in a lengthy report on tales of crashed and secretly retrieved alien spacecraft. The story concerned a woman who Cooper first crossed paths with in 1989. He described her only as a nurse, and gave her the pseudonym of "Mary." As you will see soon, that alias was not too far off from the real name of *another* nurse linked to the story. Decades ago, Cooper's informant allegedly worked at what is, today, the New Mexico-based Los Alamos National Laboratory.

* * * * * * * * * * * *

"SHE THOUGHT THEY MAY HAVE COME FROM JAPAN AFTER THE WAR"

In Cooper's own words of 1990 and which Stringfield published: "She casually mentioned to me over coffee that 'bodies' were being flown to Los Alamos periodically from late 1945 to sometime in 1947. I asked her if she had seen these 'bodies' and she said no, but others had. I asked her where these 'bodies' were coming from. She said she did not know but it was rumored that they were human experiments for biological and nuclear medicine research.

She thought they may have come from Japan after the war [italics mine]. I asked her why she thought that. She said that they were small bodies with deformed heads and limbs. The eyes were abnormally big, she was told. She did have some view of them in the morgue very briefly for a few minutes at some distance. I asked her why she was allowed to be present at the autopsies. She told me that she was asked to assist in the preparation and cleanup. I asked her again about the bodies. She said they were being flown in on special transport planes equipped with refrigerator units to keep the bodies from decomposing. The flesh was badly burned and charred. There was no hair on the heads and had a grayish-yellow color. That's all she knew."

The yellow color, you will recall, was also mentioned by Beverly Bean, in relation to the July 21, 1969 testimony of her father, Melvin Brown, who blew a very sizeable whistle when he said that the bodies he saw "could have passed for Chinese."

* * * * * * * * * * *

CATALOGING A COLLECTION

It's a little known fact that in late 2001 Tim Cooper sold all of his voluminous UFO files to Dr. Robert M. Wood. Bob is the author of *Alien Viruses* and the father of Ryan Wood who has spent years researching alleged crashed UFO incidents – all detailed in his book, *Majic Eyes Only*. It is even less well-known that in the early days of 2002, Bob hired me to spend a week in an Orange County, California-based motel-room, surrounded by all of the thousands upon thousands of pages of Cooper's voluminous collection of the cosmic sort.

The plan was for me to catalog all of the material, to compile each and every piece of it into chronological order, and to summarize the content of each document, every letter, and every Freedom of Information request that Cooper had submitted to government agencies – which is precisely what I did. It was a week in which I most definitely earned my loot. It was also a week that paralleled the infamous story told by Hunter S. Thompson in his classic gonzo saga, *Fear and Loathing in Las Vegas*. Whereas Thompson was hunkered down with his whisky, margaritas and shrimp cocktails, for me it was cases of cold beer and club sandwiches. But, I digress.

* * * * * * * * * * *

STRANGE PHONE-BASED CONVERSATIONS

Going through the vast mountain(s) of material – that for almost the entire period lay sprawled chaotically across the floor of the hotel-room – I came across several references to Cooper's elusive nurse "Mary." Mainly in letters. Those same references revealed what, at first anyway, I thought was the real name of Cooper's source: Marian Jo Ehart, of Montrose, Colorado. There was a telephone number, too, which Cooper had scribbled on a piece of paper that was torn out of a spiral notepad and which had a 1990 date on it. I wasted no time in phoning the number and spoke to a woman of that name who, after I introduced myself, responded to my questions in a very cagey and careful fashion. No, Marian was not at Los Alamos in 1947. That was certainly true. Indeed, I was able to fully verify that she was still a teenager at the time of Roswell; sixteen, to be exact. But, she definitely knew certain things relative to the matters that I brought up in the conversation – namely, those specific to Cooper's references concerning (a) deformed Japanese people held at Los Alamos; and (b) "human experiments for biological and nuclear medicine research" back in the 1940s.

From her words, I quickly deduced that Marian was not "Mary" after all. Her way-too-young age in 1947 was the clincher. As I figured out from her words to me, Marian was carefully and dutifully protecting *someone else*. It was someone who knew the truth of the Los Alamos stories and who had confided in Marian. And, probably someone who preferred to remain in the background and absolutely nowhere else. Cooper, I concluded, was carefully protecting the real source, too; he was using Marian's identity to shield *her* very own Deep Throat. To say this particular story was dominated by layer upon layer of mystery and intrigue is right on the money.

There is, however, no doubt at all that Marian did work in the field of nursing. The Colorado Licensing website reveals that Marian was "a Nursing - Intravenous Certification licensed to practice in Colorado. This licensed professional license is not current. The license was granted 01/20/1972 and expired on 10/11/2007."

In light of the fact that Marian was licensed to work as a nurse in Colorado as far back as 1972 – only twenty-five years after Roswell – it's not at all impossible that she got the story from someone else in the field of nursing; a person who *was* in a position to see the Los Alamos bodies and someone who was very likely still alive, and quietly talking, in the early 1970s.

Whatever Marian Jo Ehart *really* knew went to the grave with her. As did the name of the probable nurse she got her data from. Marian died on August 11, 2013 at the age of eighty-two and is buried in the Delta Municipal Cemetery in Delta, Colorado.

* * * * * * * * * * *

"BIZARRE BIOLOGICAL EXPERIMENTS"

It was also in 1990 that Timothy Cooper began circulating – to a limited number of colleagues and friends - a similar story to that attributed to the enigmatic Marian Ehart. This one centered on a man named Albert Collins, who was born in 1912, and who was in his late seventies when he first spoke with Cooper. During the Second World War, Collins – who graduated from the Los Angeles, California-based Occidental College in 1942 - was employed at Berkeley on the Manhattan Project. It was a highly secret program which resulted in the creation of the atomic bomb and the end of the Second World War when the Japanese cities of Nagasaki and Hiroshima were bombed into near-oblivion.

In decidedly synchronistic fashion, Collins lived in Big Bear Valley – just like Tim Cooper, and which is how the pair got to know each other. The January 10, 1991 issue of the *Big Bear Grizzly* – which covered the Big Bear Valley area – referred to Collins in his obituary as the "valley watchdog" of the area.

While cataloging all of Cooper's material for Bob Wood, I came across Cooper's original notes of his meetings with Collins. Cooper had typed Collins' words so precisely that it made me think the conversation was recorded. It may well have been, but if such a recording did exist, it wasn't contained in the material I studied and cataloged for Bob Wood. Perhaps Cooper elected to hold back on certain, choice items. It would not surprise me if that was the case.

According to Collins' words and recollections, "I saw some notes from a friend of mine. He told me that New Mexico was abuzz with unusual research into nuclear powered aircraft *and bizarre biological experiments* [italics mine]. Some people were losing their clearances for no apparent reasons...All I know is that the scary feelings everybody had who was asked to do experiments on stuff that nobody ever saw before and how we were later threatened if we talked about anything we saw, felt or heard."

Then, there was the tantalizingly brief aside Collins made to Cooper about certain autopsies in 1945 and 1947 of "...midget people with mongoloid heads that were accidentally exposed to high doses of radiation at Los Alamos."

Were these the same bodies that Marian Ehart's source referred to, *also* at Los Alamos? Probably, yes.

* * * * * * * * * * *

FROM RESEARCHER TO VICTIM

One final thing on this issue: a study of all of Cooper's files reveals something else of note. Namely, that in the period 1989-1991, Cooper was speaking with more than a few UFO researchers, and particularly so Leonard Stringfield. He also hooked up with Stan Friedman and Timothy Good – their correspondence is in the document collection, too. Cooper's material shows that in that particular period, he was busy chasing down various threads suggesting that the Roswell crash might have had at its heart a disturbing domestic origin, rather than an extraterrestrial one.

And, as the vast body of material I dug into for Bob Wood also revealed, it was *after* Cooper started poking around - in search of data and sources that could fill in the blanks of the "human experimentation" angle - that he suddenly found himself flooded with mountains of controversial and likely bogus UFO-themed files that, time-wise, far-too-conveniently emphasized the E.T. angle. Files, I might add, which were almost certainly concocted by counter-intelligence personnel, designed to steer Cooper away from secret experiments and in the direction of aliens. As I went through that strange mass of papers in an Orange County motel room in 2002, I couldn't fail to see that Cooper's files could effortlessly be cataloged in two, clear categories: the pre- and the post-questioned-document years.

Unfortunately, Cooper couldn't help but follow the E.T. path – the documents were so seductive and addictive – and it cost him, big time. From the early-to-late 1990s, Cooper was constantly tarred with claims that he, himself, faked the material, which is not the case at all. Or, that he was knowingly promoting bogus papers. On that issue, I am open-minded.

Like the people on-board the doomed Roswell craft, Cooper himself became a victim of the mysterious crash, too. Albeit, in a very different way.

11:

JOHN KEEL AND JAPANESE BALLOONS

OVER the years, there has been a small amount of Roswell-related debate on John Keel's assertion that what came down at the Foster Ranch, New Mexico in July 1947 was a Japanese Fugo balloon. In terms of what, exactly, those particular balloons were, let's take a look at what Linton Weeks noted, in a 2015 online article titled "Beware of Japanese Balloon Bombs." He wrote: "At some point during World War II, scientists in Japan figured out a way to harness a brisk air stream that sweeps eastward across the Pacific Ocean — to dispatch silent and deadly devices to the American mainland."

Weeks continued: "The project - named Fugo - 'called for sending bomb-carrying balloons from Japan to set fire to the vast forests of America, in particular those of the Pacific Northwest. It was hoped that the fires would create havoc, dampen American morale and disrupt the U.S. war effort,' James M. Powles describes in a 2003 issue of the journal World War II. The balloons, or 'envelopes,' designed by the Japanese army were made of lightweight paper fashioned from the bark of trees. Attached were bombs composed of sensors, powder-packed tubes, triggering devices and other simple and complex mechanisms."

* * * * * * * * * * *

JOHN KEEL AND ROSWELL, A TIMELINE BEGINS

In 1990, Keel outlined his theories that the Roswell wreckage came from a Fugo balloon. He did so in the pages of *Fate*, a still-popular magazine on the paranormal that has existed for decades. In Keel's own words, and in relation to the post-Second World War era, we have this: "A curtain of secrecy continued to shield the unwary public from the explosive balloons in their midst. The biggest breach of this security occurred in July 1947, at the height of the first 'flying saucer scare' when, after a severe storm, the remains of one of the balloons was found on a ranch in Lincoln County, New Mexico. Local newspapers described the find, and the wire services picked up the story. Later, military authorities carted away the materials and announced it was nothing but a 'weather balloon.' Obviously, they were determined to keep the existence of the Fugo balloons a secret two years after the war. In fact, few knew about the Fugo project until the 1950s, when a small Japanese booklet on the subject was published."

The Fugo balloons were, potentially at least, highly dangerous. The bombs they carried did, unfortunately, result in loss of life in the United States, albeit only on one occasion, in Oregon in May 1945. But, the balloons were flimsy and they were certainly not capable of carrying a human crew. Keel, however, was most definitely onto something when it came to the matter of Japanese balloons. As we have seen, in the post-war period the U.S. military acquired secret plans for new massive balloons that the Japanese were building before Hiroshima and Nagasaki were bombed, and it was these balloons that are part and parcel of the story that this book tells.

In fact, the people I interviewed for my *Body Snatchers in the Desert* book said that some of the secret 1947 flights involved gliders held aloft below massive balloon arrays. They were based on Japanese designs for what was described as a next-generation Fugos. But, most certainly, they were not the far smaller, less advanced designs that were used to attack the United States during the latter stages of the Second World War. There is, however, yet another aspect of Keel's work that definitely needs highlighting, as we shall now see.

* * * * * * * * * * * *

"THEY WOULD HAVE SELECTED THE SMALLEST, LIGHTEST VOLUNTEERS AVAILABLE"

In 1993, Keel was once again hot on the trail of Roswell's Japanese balloon. This time, however, his focus was on *manned* balloons. From 1990 to 1993, there was a deep and ongoing debate on the Roswell / Fugo matter in the pages of *Fate* magazine, with comments, observations and articles from the likes of Keel himself and Roswell authority, Kevin Randle. There is something I find very intriguing about this particular matter. Many of the people who, over the years, have commented on Keel's Fugo theory failed to note - or didn't even comment on the fact - that he also talked about uncovering data on Japanese balloons *with crews* that, allegedly, reached the U.S. in the closing stages of the war, and which - his sources said - were subject to stringent U.S. military secrecy. By crews, I mean people.

In April 1993, in an article titled "Return of the Fugos," Keel revealed that in the wake of the publicity given to his original "Roswell was a Fugo balloon" theory, he was contacted by three people who had an intriguing story to relate of certain things that occurred to them back in the 1940s, in the California desert. These same things - which took place at some point in early 1945 – concerned the sighting by all three of a low-flying balloon that had a gondola attached below it, and which, said one of the trio of witnesses, contained "a living creature."

As the balloon came closer, said Keel, the "creature" could now be seen as "a very small man wearing some kind of headgear, probably radio headphones. The poor fellow was clearly agitated… He appeared to be Oriental."

The balloon then disappeared over the horizon. No sooner as it had done so, when a couple of U.S. military jeeps quickly appeared on the scene, heading in the direction of the balloon. A few minutes later, the ominous sounds of gunshots rang out. Realizing that the group of three friends had seen or heard pretty much all that had taken place, the military returned and sternly warned them not to say anything about what they had experienced - to anybody at all. They might as well have added "or else," just to make sure the threat had left its mark.

Keel himself commented on this matter - of secret Japanese balloon-based flights to the U.S. undertaken in the latter stages of the Second World War with people on-board - as follows: "If such a project was launched, they would have selected the smallest lightest volunteers available...It is also likely they might have expired during the trip...their complexions would have been very odd, discolored by the cold…"

He concluded on this matter: "If even one such volunteer

balloonist attempted the trip and crashed, we would have the answer to all those rumors and legends which persist to this day."

On this same issue, and as I noted in my earlier book on Roswell, my sources alluded to the fact that as well as hearing of the secret domestic projects of the U.S. military which occurred in 1947, they too had heard rumors of a few examples of manned balloon-based flights to the U.S. by Japanese military personnel in the latter part of the Second World War. They were flights which ended catastrophically for the crews, who did not survive the flights for a variety of reasons, but chiefly as a result of altitude, weather, and the rigors involved in undertaking such dicey long missions.

* * * * * * * * * * *

"SMALL, ORIENTAL-LOOKING MEN IN FLIGHT SUITS"

So, we have a highly complex situation in which, just before the power of the atom brought the Second World War to a shuddering end, Japanese military personnel were making clandestine flights in large balloons to the United States – for what were clearly nefarious purposes. And we have another situation in which, just two years later, the U.S. military made use of very similar Japanese balloon-based technology, and Japanese personnel, for its own purposes. Both angles were subjected to intense secrecy, as one would imagine.

In the war, the secrecy existed so that the American public and the media would not learn that the Japanese – to an *extremely* limited degree – had made it to the United States in large balloons. Morale had to be carefully and diligently maintained. Telling the American people that the Japanese had reached the U.S. mainland

–in balloons, no less - would definitely not have been a good thing. In 1947, however, the secrecy existed to prevent the same public and media from finding out that just a couple of years after the war was over, Japan and the U.S. were in cahoots of a very controversial kind.

A few more words from Keel, who said that the reports of Japanese balloons, and particularly those with crews, "…would explain many other things, too, such as the persistent rumors in the 1940s about the bodies of small, Oriental-looking men in flight suits that were supposedly recovered in various western states."

In terms of those same "persistent rumors" to which he referred, Keel was of course, talking about tales coming out of the American southwest of dead dwarfish aliens and wrecked flying saucers. Roswell was the premier persistent rumor, with Aztec dutifully trailing behind – as it always has done to its "big brother."

In pursuing the Japanese balloon angle, John Keel came closer than many realized to the truth of the Roswell-Japan connection. Probably closer than even Keel himself ever quite realized. Keel's mistake was not that he chose to chase down the Japanese trail: he certainly got the right country. Keel's mistake was that he got *the wrong Japanese balloon*. Keel diligently went after the flimsy wartime Fugos, when he should have really been looking for the much bigger, and far sturdier, Japanese-originated balloons. They were the ones that were secretly tested in New Mexico in the summer of 1947, and which may also have been responsible for a handful of penetrations of the United States by the Japanese military in 1945, just before the war ended. Nevertheless, Keel's work was – and remains – an important part of the story you are reading.

12:

THE AIR FORCE COMES UP WITH AN ANSWER

NINETEEN-NINETY-FOUR was the year in which the UFO research community got even more fired up by Roswell. It was all due to the publication of a U.S. Air Force report on the July 1947 event. Its title was *Report of Air Force Research Regarding the Roswell Incident.* Was the government about to come clean on the issue of what happened on the Foster Ranch? Were the remains of dead aliens about to be presented to the world? Not exactly, no. In fact, the military was heading into territory that was previously unchartered.

Matters really began in the early part of 1993. That was when the late Steven Schiff – who was the Congressman for New Mexico at the time – approached the Department of Defense, seeking out the truth on the one alleged UFO case that just about everyone has heard of. Schiff mailed a letter to the Secretary of Defense at the time, Les Aspin. Schiff came right to the point and said: "Last fall I became aware of a strange series of events beginning in New Mexico over 45 years ago and involving personnel of what was then the Army Air Force. I have since reviewed the facts in some detail, and I am writing to request your assistance in arriving at a definitive explanation of what transpired and why."

Aspin chose not to reply to Schiff. That task was given to Colonel Larry G. Shockley, of the Air Force. Shockley informed Schiff that he had "referred this matter to the National Archives and Records Administration for direct reply to you."

The response from the National Archives' staff did not please Schiff or his staff: "The U.S. Air Force has retired to our custody its records on Project Blue Book relating to the investigations of unidentified flying objects. Project Blue Book has been declassified and the records are available for examination in our research room. The project closed in 1969 and we have no information after that date. We have received numerous requests concerning records relating to the Roswell incident among these records. We have not located any documentation relating to this event in Project Blue Book records, or in any other pertinent Defense Department records in our custody."

"Passing the buck" and "given the runaround" were the terms that filled Schiff's head when he got the news. It was news that he was far from satisfied with. That same runaround continued for weeks, and finally for months. By now utterly frustrated, angry and puzzled, Schiff finally chose to take another approach. It was a very ambitious move. Schiff contacted the Government Accountability Office (at the time it was known as the General Accounting Office), which is the investigative body of the U.S. Congress. The GAO wasted no time in planning to tackle the mystery. Its staff, however, were beaten to the finish-line. By whom? By the Air Force, that's who.

* * * * * * * * * * *

"THERE WAS NO DISPUTE THAT SOMETHING HAPPENED NEAR ROSWELL IN JULY 1947"

Although the USAF maintained that it held no records on Roswell, when word got out that the GAO was now on the hunt for the truth behind the Foster Ranch incident, the Air Force quickly launched its very own investigation. The result of that same investigation was the publication of the aforementioned July 1994 *Report of Air Force Research Regarding the Roswell Incident*. It would be another year before the GAO's conclusions were revealed, on July 28, 1995.

The GAO's National Security and International Affairs Division wrote in their finished dossier: "DOD [Department of Defense] informed us that the U.S. Air Force report of July 1994, entitled *Report of Air Force Research Regarding the Roswell Incident*, represents the extent of DOD records or information concerning the Roswell crash. "

The GAO continued: "The Air Force report concluded that there was no dispute that something happened near Roswell in July 1947 and that all available official material indicated the most likely source of the wreckage recovered was one of the project MOGUL balloon trains. At the time of the Roswell crash, project MOGUL was a highly classified U.S. effort to determine the state of Soviet nuclear weapons research using balloons that carried radar reflectors."

The Mogul theory is the one which is still endorsed by the U.S. Air Force to this day. It should be noted, however, that not a single shred of documentation has ever surfaced from the Air Force's archives and which *conclusively* proves that the Roswell debris was from a Mogul balloon train. The Mogul theory was, and still is, simply that – a theory and nothing else.

The mainstream media pretty much accepted the explanation of the Air Force, which was the predictable outcome: UFOs rarely attract the serious attention of respected investigative journalists. UFOlogists, meanwhile, rolled their collective eyes, unsatisfied with anything that wasn't completely pro-UFO in nature. That was pretty much predictable too. As for the GAO, well, behind the scenes its staff were privately puzzled – even angry in some quarters – by the fact that the Air Force had effectively jumped the gun. And that is certainly accurate terminology.

What the Air Force was *supposed* to have done was to offer any and all assistance that it could to the Government Accountability Office and to hand over copies of any and all relevant Roswell-based documentation in its possession. This was the same for each and every other agency which the GAO approached, too. The list included the FBI, the National Security Agency, the Department of Defense, and the CIA. That the Air Force hastily launched its *own* investigation, published a report, and quickly shot down any and all explanations beyond Project Mogul, made many people within UFOlogy conclude that the Air Force was engaging in a sizeable amount of what is commonly known as "damage control."

There are clear indications that Congressman Schiff had his suspicions that he had not been given the full, true story of what occurred at Roswell. His beef, however, was not with the GAO. In fact Schiff personally praised the agency, calling its work on the Roswell case "professional, conscientious and thorough." What Schiff was *not* happy with, were the eye-opening revelations that a massive number of records from the old Roswell Army Air Field could not be found. Not here. Not there. Not *anywhere*.

Schiff told the press: "It is my understanding that these outgoing messages were permanent records which should never have been destroyed. The GAO could not identify who destroyed the messages, or why."

This is an issue we will return to in the next chapter.

* * * * * * * * * * *

THE AIR FORCE PAYS CAVITT A VISIT

One of the primary reasons why the Air Force felt that the Mogul balloon scenario worked so well was because of the sheer scale of the arrays. They were *gigantic* clusters of balloons. In that sense, the Project Mogul balloons could, theoretically, have explained the presence of the huge debris field on the Foster Ranch – a field of debris that clearly could not have been caused by anything as insignificant as a small, solitary weather-balloon.

It's ironic, however, that one of the primary Roswell players – and who the U.S. Air Force spoke with, hoping he would add weight to their Project Mogul argument – completely failed to take the bait. On the matter of the nature of the debris, he would have nothing at all to do with the Mogul program. That man was one of the very few people that just about everyone who has studied the Roswell controversy agrees was definitely on-site when the materials were found and recovered: Sheridan Cavitt, formerly of the Counter-Intelligence Corps.

On May 24, 1994, Colonel Richard L. Weaver, USAF – who, at the time, was the Air Force's Director of Security and Special Program Oversight – interviewed Cavitt at Cavitt's home. Mary, Cavitt's wife, was also present throughout the interview. In its published report, the Air Force had some intriguing things to say about Cavitt and his comments on the Roswell event. There is an important reason why I have reproduced, below, a section of the Cavitt interview. That reason will become apparent imminently. The USAF said, in its 1994 report and prefacing the interview:

* * * * * * * * * * *

"HE IS SOMETIMES PORTRAYED AS A CLOSED-MOUTH (OR SOMETIMES EVEN SINISTER) CONSPIRATOR"

"Cavitt is credited in all claims of having accompanied Major Marcel to the ranch to recover the debris, sometimes along with his Counter Intelligence Corps (CIC) subordinate, William Rickett, who, like Marcel, is deceased. Although there does not appear to be much dispute that Cavitt was involved in the material recovery, other claims about him prevail in the popular literature. He is sometimes portrayed as a closed-mouth (or sometimes even sinister) conspirator who was one of the early individuals who kept the 'secret of Roswell' from getting out. Other things about him have been alleged, including the claim that he wrote a report of the incident at the time that has never surfaced."

In view of the above, it's not at all surprising that the Air Force wanted to speak with Cavitt. The USAF report continues:

> "Since Lt. Col. Cavitt, who had first-hand knowledge, was still alive, a decision was made to interview him and get a signed sworn statement from him about his version of the events. Prior to the interview, the Secretary of the Air Force provided him with a written authorization and waiver to discuss classified information with the interviewer and release him from any security oath he may have taken. Subsequently, Cavitt was interviewed on May 24, 1994, at his home. Cavitt provided a signed, sworn statement of his recollections in this matter. He also consented to having the interview tape-recorded.

"In this interview, Cavitt related that he had been contacted on numerous occasions by UFO researchers and had willingly talked with many of them; however, he felt that he had oftentimes been misrepresented or had his comments taken out of context so that their true meaning was changed. He stated unequivocally, however, that the material he recovered consisted of a reflective sort of material like aluminum foil, and some thin, bamboo-like sticks. He thought at the time, and continued to do so today, that what he found was a weather balloon and has told other private researchers that.

"He also remembered finding a small 'black box' type of instrument, which he thought at the time was probably a radiosonde. Lt. Col. Cavitt also reviewed the famous Ramey/Marcel photographs of the wreckage taken to Ft. Worth and he identified the materials depicted in those photos as consistent with the materials that he recovered from the ranch. Lt. Col. Cavitt also stated that he had never taken any oath or signed any agreement not to talk about this incident and had never been threatened by anyone in the government because of it. He did not even know the incident was claimed to be anything unusual until he was interviewed in the early 1980's."

Cavitt told Colonel Weaver:

"...I couldn't swear to the dates, but in that time, which must have been July, we heard that someone had found some debris out not to far from Roswell and it looked

> suspicious; it was unidentified. So, I went out and I do not recall whether Marcel went with Rickett and me; I had Rickett with me. We went out to his site. There were no, as I understand, checkpoints or anything like that (going through guards and that sort of garbage) we went out there and we found it. It was a small amount of, as I recall, bamboo sticks, reflective sort of material that would, well at first glance, you would probably think it was aluminum foil, something of that type. And we gathered up some of it."

Cavitt had more to say:

> "I don't know where we even tried to get all of it. It wasn't scattered, well, what I would call, you know, extensively. Like it didn't go along the ground and splatter off some here and some there. We gathered up some of it and took it back to the base and I remember I had turned it over to Marcel. As I say, I do not remember whether Marcel was there or not on the site. He could have been. We took it back to the intelligence room in the CIC office."

* * * * * * * * * * *

"SOME SORT OF BALLOON?"

The Air Force's statement is notable for not just what it says, but also for what it does *not* say. The USAF report makes it clear that in Cavitt's opinion, what he saw and picked up was weather-balloon debris. From one single balloon. Not more than one balloon. And definitely not an array of balloons. Given that the materials used in both weather-balloons and Mogul balloons were essentially one and the same, that meant the ball was still just about in the Air Force's court: the Mogul theory still held water, and one of the last-surviving people who were at the crash-site was endorsing it. Well, no, he wasn't. The exact opposite, actually.

The most important document in this aspect of the Roswell puzzle is not the Air Force's 1994 report, but its massive 1995 publication / behemoth, *The Roswell Report: Fact Vs Fiction in the New Mexico Desert*, a copy of which was mailed to me by Colonel Weaver when it was published. It runs to more than 1,000 pages. Unlike the far slimmer 1994 report, the huge 1995 USAF document contains a full transcript of the interview between Colonel Weaver and Cavitt.

The report shows that Colonel Weaver asked Cavitt: "... when you went out and saw this material, there was no doubt in your mind that it was some sort of man-made material? And, you thought at the time was a weather balloon, some sort of balloon?"

Cavitt replied: "When I first saw it," implying to the colonel that he knew immediately it was balloon debris. Now we get to the important part.

Colonel Weaver continued with his questioning and asked Cavitt how big the debris field was. Cavitt's response: "Maybe as long as this room is wide."

The colonel asked for clarification on Cavitt's words : "So, twenty feet maybe?"

Cavitt said, as he pointed around the room: "Some here, some here, some here. No concentration of it."

* * * * * * * * * * *

WHEN SIZE - AND PARTICULARLY THE LACK OF IT - REALLY MATTERS

That all brings us to the biggest problem in this aspect of the overall Roswell debate: almost no one of significance in the Roswell story disputes that the debris field on the ranch was expansive. Even the Air Force believed that. It still does, if asked. And, the fact that the field *was* so huge, and packed with debris allowed the USAF to make a somewhat plausible case that it came from one of the military's goliath-sized Mogul arrays. But, when talking to Colonel Weaver in 1994, Cavitt *outright disputed* the size of the field. It was, he said, just about "as long as this room is wide."

Cavitt's testimony was *potentially* extremely important to the Air Force, as it could have helped bolster the idea that the materials came from Project Mogul. But, Cavitt's words on the size of the area in which the material was found, were wholly inconsistent with what one would expect to see if Mogul was the culprit. Instead, what Cavitt described was consistent with just a small weather-balloon: not much wreckage and a very small area in which the materials were strewn about. On top of that, when Colonel Weaver brought up the matter of Project Mogul, Cavitt shot back: "Never heard of it."

Perplexing is the fact that the USAF never addressed that one notable inconsistency: how could Project Mogul have been the culprit when, according to Cavitt – who even the Air Force accepts was at the ranch in July 1947 with Bill Rickett - the amount of material found would have fitted comfortably in his and Mary's living-room?

In an August 1995 article titled "*The Roswell Incident* and *Project Mogul*," written for the *Skeptical Inquirer*, Dave Thomas said of the Mogul balloons, "Some of these flights consisted of very long trains containing up to two dozen neoprene sounding balloons, *having a total length of more than 600 feet* [italics mine]."

Does that sound, to you, like something which could have comfortably fitted inside one room of the Cavitt home? Remember, the Cavitt's living-room was not large. When asked about the size of the debris field, Cavitt told Colonel Weaver it was no longer than the width of the room in which the interview was then taking place. To which Weaver asked, "so, twenty feet maybe?"

Cavitt made not a single attempt to dispute Colonel Weaver's math.

Good luck trying to shovel 600-feet of Mogul-based balloon materials into a twenty-foot-wide room.

* * * * * * * * * * * *

SWORN TO SECRECY VS NOT SWORN TO SECRECY

There is something else, too: if Cavitt knew all along that what he, Marcel and Rickett saw and collected came from a weather-balloon, why then did Cavitt – or all three of them – not nip things in the bud and lay matters to rest before the "flying disc" statement was released to the media? The Air Force's only theory on this issue goes as follows: "...it seems that that there was overreaction by Colonel Blanchard and Major Marcel in originally reporting that a 'flying disc' had been recovered when, at that time, nobody knew for sure what that term meant, since it had only been in use for a couple of weeks."

That statement does make some sense – after all, flying saucer hysteria was definitely growing, as it was only two weeks earlier that pilot Kenneth Arnold launched the era of UFOs. That Cavitt was so adamant that he *immediately* knew the material was from a weather-balloon still means he could have quashed everything before it erupted.

Also, Colonel Weaver's report makes it clear he was familiar with the testimony of the RAAF's Provost Marshal, Major Edwin Easley, who had told Kevin Randle that with respect to Roswell, he was sworn to secrecy. Easley died in 1992, but no attempt was ever made by the USAF to address his revelations.

Recall that the Air Force stated, "prior to the interview [with Cavitt], the Secretary of the Air Force provided him with a written authorization and waiver to discuss classified information with the interviewer and release him from any security oath he may have taken."

Cavitt was not too bothered by this, as he made it clear to Colonel Weaver that he "was not sworn into secrecy ever about any of this stuff."

That, unlike Cavitt, Easley was adamant *he* had signed a secrecy oath is surely something that should have caught the attention of the USAF. And, more importantly, the Air Force *knew* Easley had made such a statement. That this important matter was not chased down can only be described as troubling.

My well-worn copy of the U.S. Air Force's 1995 report on Roswell (Nick Redfern)

* * * * * * * * * * *

COVER-UP OR AN HONEST QUEST FOR THE TRUTH?

My view on all this? I believe that, just like John Keel, the Air Force was absolutely right to go looking for a balloon-driven program. As I see it, that is where all of the evidence points. But, also like Keel, the USAF got the wrong kind of balloon. It wasn't a weather-balloon. It wasn't a Fugo balloon. It wasn't even one of the gargantuan Mogul affairs. As one of my original sources told me years ago: there is no better way to hide a classified balloon-based operation than by hiding it behind *another* classified balloon-based operation. Mogul, then, may have been the convenient fall-guy for a project that was far more controversial in nature; a project of sinister proportions and which was also inextricably linked to new and novel balloons flown in the skies of New Mexico in 1947.

Was the Air Force of 1994 hiding the history of a series of post-war human experiments behind something else, such as Mogul? Or, incredibly, was the truth hidden from the Air Force, too? Do I think the Air Force engaged in chicanery, lying and obfuscation? Did the Air Force make a legitimate search, only to find little at all? These are all important questions.

Personally, I think the USAF legitimately went looking, but in doing so found nothing of a smoking-gun nature in the slightest. So, its investigators continued to search, finally focusing on Mogul, and coming to accept that without definitive documentation to make a cast-iron case, the whole thing was destined to remain a ufological equivalent of Jack the Ripper. Namely, an old mystery, one that was filled with intrigue, but which was lacking in a definitive answer. Perceiving quite correctly and astutely that coming up with no answer, at all, was unacceptable, the Air Force went with the only candidate that it thought made at least some degree of sense: Project Mogul.

Based on the words of my sources, I am as certain as I can be that either (a) the relevant files were destroyed decades ago (which would explain why the Air Force of 1994 came up with nothing solid), or (b) the documentation was locked away – also decades ago – to prevent a dirty secret from ever leaking out and embarrassing not just the Air Force, but the entire U.S. Government, and even the President.

If the former is the correct scenario, we may forever be reliant on nothing more than the old memories of equally old people who are now nearly all gone. If the latter proves to be accurate, however, there is still a chance we might one day get our hands on the elusive proof: documents, photos, autopsy reports, and so on. If that happens, I predict the Air Force of 1994 will be shown to have been out of the loop, but not sinister conspirators.

As for Cavitt, was he carrying out some kind of secret duty right up until the very end? Was he – even as late as the 1990s – still answerable to someone else? Was it the same person, or agency, Bill Rickett was still so concerned about crossing? Someone above the Air Force and the GAO? Someone concerned that, if the USAF kept pushing for answers, the hidden truth might still surface? Was Cavitt, by maintaining the weather-balloon scenario, even determined to keep the hidden facts out of the hands of Colonel Weaver? Quite possibly.

Tony Bragalia notes of Cavitt: "His lawyer-son Joseph Cavitt said his father would get angry whenever the Roswell incident was brought up. He said his father had 'issues' and that 'it was like having half of a father.'" Equally intriguing, Bragalia added that

Cavitt "refused pain medication at the end of his life, afraid he would talk."

Obviously, there was no need for Cavitt to avoid taking pain meds in case he spoke about as something as innocuous as a weather-balloon – or even a Mogul balloon, which was comprised of basically the same materials as a weather-balloon. To his dying day, it seems, Cavitt chose not to reveal the secret he kept for so long.

It seems, however, there was a great deal that Cavitt *could* have said, had he chose to. For example, Kevin Randle interviewed Sheridan Cavitt on January 29, 1990. Randle notes of their exchange: "During that interview, [Cavitt] was only nervous once and that was when we began talking about the bodies. He looked at me, leaned forward and picked up a magazine, sat back, tossed the magazine to the table and asked 'Bill Rickett tell you that?'"

Randle continued: "When I said, 'No,' Cavitt visibly relaxed."

* * * * * * * * * * *

"OR EVEN WORSE, CAPTURED JAPANESE PRISONERS"

It's notable that 1994 was also the year in which *UFO* magazine waded into the controversy of Roswell. You might think that its staff were thinking of things from an alien perspective. You would be quite wrong. At the time, Vicki Ecker was the editor of the publication. She wrote:

> "A favorite knee-jerk comment aimed at anyone even lightly prone to conspiratorial thinking is this reliable old saw: 'But everyone knows the government can't keep secrets!' Well, the recent horrifying disclosures about

> America's nuclear tests during the Cold War roundly put the lie to that. Hundreds – perhaps thousands – of innocent people were victimize by scientists and military who hid the truth about the effects of nuclear substances on the human body. Shades of those hideous Nazi experiments! And more such secret tests are undoubtedly tucked away. What if the Roswell crash was a failed nuclear experiment – either ours or someone else's? The site was not found to be radioactive, the answer comes back. Well then, perhaps it wasn't nuclear, but if it was, that aspect has bene kept secret. Maybe it was still a test of some kind, using shaved monkeys – *or even worse, captured Japanese prisoners, for instance – as experimental passengers on an ill-fated flight. Ergo, 'alien bodies'* [Italics mine]."

Ecker added:

> "It's even possible that some secret technological advances had brought into existence a remarkably thin but unbendable, unbreakable metal substance a la... Roswell debris. The concept of casting molten steel into very thin sheets, after all, dates back to the mid-nineteenth century. 'Now, I ask,' one conspiratorial thinker rightly asks, 'Which scenario is more plausible? A visitor from outer space? Or experiments conducted by our government?'"

They are questions well worth pondering on – regardless of whether or not they appeal to you or have a bearing on your belief-systems.

13:

A DESTRUCTION OF FILES

ON July 28, 1995, the Government Accountability Office's report on the Roswell affair surfaced from its National Security and International Affairs Division. The GAO's report did not provide any smoking guns – such as old black and white photos of dead bodies and wreckage at the crash-site on the Foster Ranch, New Mexico. The report did, however, provide something interesting and controversial. And it's something that has been misinterpreted for years.

During the course of their search for records to try and better understand what had taken place at Roswell in early July 1947, the GAO learned that the entire outgoing messages from the Roswell Army Air Field generated during the period that the event occurred were *missing. Vanished. Gone.* And under circumstances that could not be fully determined and proved. Nor could the year in which the files went missing be confirmed. Maybe the late-forties. Maybe the fifties. The seventies? Twenty-four hours before Colonel Weaver went looking? Who knows?

This, inevitably and very understandably, led certain Roswell researchers to proclaim that this was evidence of a significant event of UFO proportions having occurred. An event which certain elements of officialdom were determined to keep forever hidden from the populace, the media, and the UFO research community - and possibly, even, from anyone else in government who might dare to come looking, such as investigators of the GAO.

Maybe, that's precisely what happened. But, the story is not quite as straightforward as that. Matters are seldom straightforward when it comes to Roswell.

* * * * * * * * * * *

THE PROBLEM OF DISAPPEARANCE

Time and again, I have heard UFO researchers say, words to the effect of: "Because the 1947 files are missing, this must mean the government or the Air Force pulled them years ago, so no-one could get the files on the aliens." Sure, that's not impossible. But, there is another issue. The files in question that are unavailable to us do not cover just the key period of the Roswell affair. Rather, they extend as far back as March 1945 and as late as 1950.

We are led to believe that if aliens crashed a couple of hours' drive from Roswell, then it was an event that occurred out of the blue, with little or no advance notice, and certainly not something that had been anticipated for a significant period of time. So, that being the case, why the need to pull files from as early as March 1945 to hide something that is said to have occurred, without much warning (*if any at all*), in the summer of 1947?

Proponents of the notion that aliens crashed not too far from the city of Roswell might say that the government was just being overly careful, and wanted to make sure that (a) nothing was left behind, and (b) nothing had been misplaced in an earlier collection of material, or indeed, within a later collection of material, possibly held in secure safes at the base. So they chose the best and quickest option available to them and scooped up pretty much everything that covered approximately two years or so before, and up to two-and-a-half years after the crash. And maybe that is exactly what happened.

On the other hand, one can make a valid argument that the vanished files issue has no bearing on Roswell from an extraterrestrial perspective, because the documents that are missing include papers dating from two years before the event even took place. This also offers a theory (and granted that's all it is) that there was another reason for the large scale loss of material that the GAO sought to uncover. Let's see what the GAO had to say about this matter of missing messages in its 1995 report:

* * * * * * * * * * * *

"MANY OF THE AIR FORCE ORGANIZATIONAL RECORDS COVERING THIS TIME PERIOD WERE DESTROYED"

> "In addition to unit history reports, we also searched for other government records on the Roswell crash. In this regard, the Chief Archivist for the National Personnel Records Center provided us with documentation indicating that (1) RAAF records such as finance and accounting, supplies, buildings and grounds, and other general administrative matters from March 1945 through December 1949 and (2) RAAF outgoing messages from October 1946 through December 1949 were destroyed."

When the GAO demanded to know the reasons behind this development, they got an answer, as GAO files note:

> "According to this official [the Chief Archivist for the National Personnel Records Center], the document disposition form did not properly indicate the authority under which the disposal action was taken. The Center's Chief Archivist stated that from his personal experience, many of the Air Force organizational records covering this time period were destroyed without entering a citation for the governing disposition authority. Our review of records control forms showing the destruction of other records - including outgoing RAAF messages for 1950 - supports the Chief Archivist's viewpoint."

So in other words, we have yet another explanation that does not include high-level conspiracy to explain the loss and destruction of files, but which says far more about bureaucracy. So what's my point in all this? Well, *this* is my point: Yes, it certainly is intriguing that half-a-decade of certain files are missing from the old Roswell Army Air Field, and it may even be an issue of deep conspiracy to hide the remains of dead aliens and their craft.

Or, it may not be.

* * * * * * * * * * *

SIX YEARS ERASED FROM HISTORY

If UFO / Roswell researchers wish to maintain that the missing files from 1947 point to a cover-up of the Roswell event - and Roswell occurred out of the blue in July of that year - then they have to provide a viable reason as to why documentation dating back as far as March 1945 was pulled too, and why additional documentation remains missing from as late as 1950. Saying that "the outgoing Roswell messages from July 1947 are missing" is absolutely true. It opens eyes and it catches the attention of UFOlogists and Roswell disciples everywhere. Noting that in reality, the files actually cover 1945 to 1950 and also cover general administrative issues at the base, is far less attention-grabbing.

Ironically, the fact that the files which have vanished (files which *still* cannot be found) span 1945 to 1950, actually adds weight to the idea that Roswell was a military experiment. Just about everyone I spoke with while writing *Body Snatchers in the Desert* told me that the human experimentation began in 1945 and ended in the late 1940s – with a few additional tests having occurred in the early fifties.

Pulling 1945-era files for a one-off event that didn't occur until the summer of 1947 makes zero sense. Pulling certain 1945-era files that might have compromised the handful of *pre*-Roswell experiments – had they reached the public domain, of course - makes *perfect* sense. The same goes for the decision to make the 1948-1950 files vanish too. The fact is that *six years* of files are missing, not just files from the time of the Roswell crash. This is indicative of a fairly lengthy series of ongoing tests that had to be hidden – not the out-of-the-blue crash of one solitary alien spacecraft midway through 1947.

It should also be recalled that President Clinton's Advisory Committee on Human Radiation Experiments revealed that "*...a number of potentially important collections could not be located and were evidently lost or destroyed* [italics mine]. Similarly, the Committee reveals, a number of those same document collections related to experiments undertaken in the fields of biomedicine, defense and space exploration; and in the great majority of these cases only fragmentary data remained. Where programs were legitimately kept secret for national security reasons, states the Committee, *the government often did not create or maintain adequate records* [italics mine], thereby preventing the public, and those most at risk, from learning the facts in a timely and complete fashion."

All of this is highly suggestive of an agenda to make Roswell go away – permanently.

14:

DUMMIES IN THE DESERT

IT'S hardly surprising that 1997 was the year in which the Roswell affair reached its pinnacle. It was, after all, the 50th anniversary of the mysterious event. Just about everyone who was anyone in UFOlogy was commenting on, or writing about, the case – mostly from the perspective of promoting and championing the alien angle. That was not the case for *exactly* everyone, however. Three years after the 1994 "Mogul Report" was published, the Air Force made a surprising acknowledgement that the reported sightings of strange bodies at Roswell *did* have a basis in fact. Not only that: so compelled by then was the Air Force to address the bodies issue that it authorized the release of yet *another* report on Roswell. The last word, lo and behold, was not the last word. The last word was *not* even in sight.

Entitled *The Roswell Report: Case Closed*, it did very little – if anything at all - to dampen the notoriety surrounding the case, however. In fact, the question of *why* the Air Force had concluded there was a pressing need on its part to explain the reports of unusual bodies found in New Mexico (when it could quite easily have summarily dismissed them as hoaxes or modern-day folklore), arguably only heightened the interest in what did or did not occur.

* * * * * * * * * * *

"I DON'T KNOW WHAT THEY SAW IN '47"

The Air Force report focused practically all of its 231 pages on the alleged recovery of the strange bodies and asserted that, "'aliens' observed in the New Mexico desert were probably anthropomorphic test dummies that were carried aloft by U.S. Air Force high altitude balloons for scientific research. The 'unusual' military activities in the New Mexico desert were high altitude research balloon launch and recovery operations. The reports of military units that always seemed to arrive shortly after the crash of a flying saucer to retrieve the saucer and 'crew,' were actually accurate descriptions of Air Force personnel engaged in anthropomorphic dummy recovery operations."

There is no doubt (it is, actually, a matter of historical record) that the Air Force conducted a wide array of tests using crash test dummies in New Mexico and that at least some of these tests did occur in the vicinities of both the White Sands Proving Ground and the town of Roswell. But were those same tests responsible – either in part or in whole – for the stories concerning highly unusual-looking bodies recovered by the military during the summer of 1947? At the time of its release, the conclusions of the Air Force's latest (final...?) report provoked a furor of controversy. While there is absolutely no doubt that tests utilizing anthropomorphic dummies were widespread in New Mexico, the Air Force's report largely and very carefully glosses over the fact that these particular tests did not even commence until the early 1950s.

This was an issue not lost on the mainstream media during the Air Force's press conference at the Pentagon which accompanied the release of the report in July 1997. A reporter asked, "How do you square the UFO enthusiasts saying that they're talking about 1947, and you're talking about dummies used in the 50's, almost a decade later?"

Air Force spokesman, Colonel John Haynes replied, slightly and noticeably awkwardly: "Well, I'm afraid that's a problem that we have with time compression. I don't know what they saw in '47, but I'm quite sure it probably was Project Mogul. But I think if you find that people talk about things over a period of time, they begin to lose exactly when the date was."

For the record, "time compression" was the 1990s equivalent of what we now know and loathe as, ahem, "alternative facts."

* * * * * * * * * * *

"A JAPANESE COUNTERPART TO OPERATION PAPERCLIP"

Another source that promoted a non-E.T-driven theory for Roswell in 1997 was *Popular Mechanics* magazine. Notably, its staff were focusing on a theory that was not at all dissimilar to the one which appeared in my *Body Snatchers in the Desert* book. To say it was near-identical would not be an exaggeration. In the July 1997 edition of the magazine, there appeared an article titled "Roswell Plus 50." It was penned by a journalist named James Wilson. According to Wilson, *Popular Mechanics* had been "alerted" to a then-forthcoming declassification of documents that might go a significant way towards finally resolving Roswell. Who, exactly, was behind the alerting was not revealed. This new story was not, however, a nod in the direction of the crash-test dummy saga. Or even a Mogul balloon. It was heading down a path towards something far more controversial, the kind of controversy that no one "in the know" wanted investigating and / or exposing.

Wilson told his readers that "the documents scheduled for future release will tell of a Japanese counterpart to Operation Paperclip. One of its purposes was to determine if the Japanese had constructed a suicide-piloted version of the Fugo incendiary bomb."

Wilson continued it was the opinion of *Popular Mechanics* that "the craft that crashed at Roswell will eventually be identified as either a U.S. attempt to re-engineer a second-generation Fugo, or a hybrid craft which uses both Fugo lifting technology and Horten-inspired lifting-body. In either case, Japanese engineers and pilots brought to the U.S. after the war to work on the project could have been the dead 'alien' bodies recovered at the crash site."

Ultimately, the Japanese-themed documents to which Wilson referred remained buried. The whole mysterious saga made me seriously wonder if there was a secret war going on within the world of the military and the intelligence community – with one side trying to get the truth out about Roswell and the other side steadfastly determined to ensure it never reached the light of day. I still think, today, that may well be the case.

And finally, that there was a Horten-UFO connection is not a matter of any doubt. On this matter of the Horten brothers, we should note the following Air Force report of January 3, 1952 – on the subject of flying saucer sightings investigated by the Air Force in the late 1940s and early 1950s. Brigadier General W.M. Garland stated something to General John A. Samford, the Air Force Director of Intelligence, which makes this connection abundantly clear by touching upon the work of the Horten brothers:

> "It is logical to relate the reported sightings to the known development of aircraft, jet propulsion, rockets and range extension capabilities in Germany and the USSR. In this connection, it is to be noted that certain developments by the Germans, *particularly the Horten wing* [italics mine], jet propulsion, and refueling, combined with their extensive employment of V-1 and V-2 weapons during World War II, lend credence to the possibility that the flying objects may be of German and Russian origin."

So yes, there was a Horten connection to the UFO mystery – we're just not fully sure of the scope of that connection. Yet.

15:

A MAN NAMED CORSO

A particularly controversial, even mysterious, player who surfaced in 1997 was the late Lieutenant Colonel Philip J. Corso, who with Bill Birnes (of the now-defunct television show, *UFO Hunters*), wrote one of the most hotly-debated books in the history of UFOlogy. Its title was: *The Day After Roswell.* According to Corso, while working with the U.S. Army's Foreign Technology Division in the early 1960s, he personally handled much of the supposed alien technology retrieved at the Foster Ranch. More controversially, according to Corso he didn't just see and handle the materials – he secretly oversaw a project to share the technology with some of the United States' most powerful companies involved in the research and production of advanced technology. Corso claimed that such technologies as fiber-optics, transistors, night-vision goggles, and certain computer-based materials were all given significant kick-starts thanks to those who studied and – to a degree – somehow managed to replicate the extraterrestrial discoveries.

According to Corso, he saw one of the Roswell bodies at Fort Riley, Kansas in the summer of 1947. He recalled: "At first I thought it was a dead child they were shipping somewhere. But this was no child. It was a four-foot human shaped figure with arms, bizarre-looking four-fingered hands - I didn't see a thumb - thin legs and feet, and an oversized incandescent lightbulb shaped head that looked like it was floating over a balloon gondola for a chin."

Corso added: "I allowed myself more time to look at the creature than I should have, I suppose, because that night I missed the time checks on the rest of my rounds and believed I'd have to come up with a pretty good explanation for the lateness of my other stops to verify the sentry assignments. But what I was looking at was worth any trouble I'd get into the next day. This thing was truly fascinating and at the same time utterly horrible. It challenged every conception I had, and I hoped against hope that I was looking at some form of atomic human mutation. I knew I couldn't ask anybody about it, and because I hoped I would never see its like again, I came up with explanation after explanation for its existence, despite what I'd read on the enclosed document: It was shipped here from Hiroshima, it was the result of a Nazi genetic experiment, it was a dead circus freak, it was anything but what I knew it said it was - what it had to be: an extraterrestrial."

For some in UFOlogy, the Corso-Birnes book was just what they wanted to hear. Others, meanwhile, thought that the whole thing was just too good to be true. As for the Air Force, it kept silent on the matter – respectfully or angrily, we don't know. There can be little doubt, though, that the Pentagon found itself in a *very* awkward position. After all, at the very same time that one of their own – Corso – was championing the alien side of the story, the Air Force was doing all that it possibly could to convince people that crash-test dummies were responsible for much of the talk of aliens.

With that said, it's time to address the life and career of a certain Major General Charles Willoughby – who just happened to be a good friend and colleague of Corso.

* * * * * * * * * * *

"THE INFORMATION PROCURED WILL HAVE THE GREATEST VALUE"

According to Tien-wei Wu (who wrote "A Preliminary Review of Studies of Japanese Biological Warfare and Unit 731 in the United States"): "Maj. Gen. Charles Willoughby, MacArthur's intelligence chief, *was in charge of the whole affair of Unit 731* [italics mine], shielding its former members from any outside contact in order to avoid any research data on biological warfare fallen into the Soviet hands. Despite the fact that Lt. Col. Thomas H. Morrow (a lawyer from Ohio) of International Prosecution Section of the Tokyo Trial and David N. Sutton, head of its Document Division, made a trip to China to collect evidence on Japanese waging biological warfare in China, during the afternoon of August 29, 1946 no sooner was the Unit 731 case raised than it was dropped. MacArthur was empowered 'to approve, reduce or otherwise alter any sentence imposed by 'the International Military Tribunal the Far East.'"

Similarly, on August 15, 2005, the *Japan Times* ran an article on Unit 731 and Willoughby. One month later, the *American Thinker* website stated, while commenting on the *Japan Times* story: "The *Japan Times* editorial says Brigadier General Charles Willoughby, head of the intelligence unit of the Occupation forces in Japan was behind Washington's efforts to gain access to Unit 731's biological and chemical research: In the documents, Willoughby described the achievements of his unit's investigations, saying the 'information procured will have the greatest value in future development of the U.S. BW (bacteria warfare) program.'

> "Citing a U.S. War Department specialist in charge of the investigation, Willoughby wrote in the report that data on human experiments may prove invaluable and the information was only obtainable through the skillful, psychological approach to top - flight pathologists involved in Unit 731 experiments. The U.S. provided money, food, gifts, entertainment and other kinds of rewards to the former Unit 731 members, according to the report. According to Keiichi Tsuneishi, a professor at Kanagawa University and an expert on biological and chemical weapons who uncovered the documents at the U.S. National Archives, members of 731 were forced by Washington to choose between cooperating and facing war crime charges."

* * * * * * * * * * *

THE CORSO-WILLOUGHBY CONNECTION

Willoughby would surely have been aware of the disturbing things going on in New Mexico in the postwar era, as they related to Unit 731, his baby, so to speak. Certainly, when I spoke with the Colonel in 2003, he said: "After [Major General Charles] Willoughby and [General] MacArthur began moves to grab the [Unit] 731 discoveries, this was seen as a 'go' signal, and the bodies and the people were all brought here, secretly brought to Los Alamos first and then a location in Chicago. No-one wanted to say it or be the first, but there was a tremendous potential to using these people. The gains in aviation medicine, nuclear medicine [and] biological warfare were huge."

So what does all of this have to do with Lt. Col. Philip Corso? The answer is quite a lot. A huge amount, one might say. Willoughby and Corso were very close and worked together in more than a few fields. In *They Cast No Shadows*, Brian Desborough reveals how following an anti-communist seminar in Mexico City in 1957, an organization was spawned called Liberty Lobby. Desborough further noted that the group ran "under the direction of Willis Carto, whose mentor, Francis Yockey, had been jailed as a Nazi sympathizer during WWII. Curiously, the steering committee of Liberty Lobby included such people as Lt. Colonel Philip Corso and Major General Charles Willoughby."

The pair was also part of a group known as the Armed Services Committee of the Sovereign Order of Saint John of Jerusalem. On top of that, Corso received a 1945 briefing on the work of Unit 731 as a part of his work undertaken for Operation Paperclip.

In *Confessions of an Illuminati*, Leo Lyon Zagami reveals that in the immediate period after President John F. Kennedy was assassinated on November 22, 1963, Corso and a man named Frank Capell (an editor for the John Birch Society) were "instrumental in spreading stories linking Oswald to Russia and Ruby to Castro's Cuba."

Zagami also notes that Corso was a member of the Armed Forces Committee of the Shickshinny Knights of Malta. He adds: "Psychological Warfare and Propaganda, including, of course, disinfo operations, were the main areas of interest for these global manipulators working for the Committee during the Cold War."

* * * * * * * * * * * *

"HIS INFORMATION MIGHT NOT HAVE BEEN THE BEST"

As we have seen, Corso was a close colleague of, and a good friend to, Major General Charles Willoughby, who just happened to be one of the key figures in the top secret operation to bring the Unit 731 people and records to the United States. The pair are known to have shared secret intelligence data. Corso was an expert in the field of disinformation – namely, creating faked stories to fool certain targets, individuals and entire countries. And, maybe, to fool the field of UFOlogy. Perhaps Corso's final, crowning glory of the fabricated kind came in 1997 with *The Day After Roswell.*

On the matter of Corso's reliability (or the lack of it), the following words of Kevin Randle – the most respected and grounded of all the various Roswell investigators within the UFO research community – are worth noting: "...when Corso came into conflict with other witnesses or information [on Roswell] that was contrary to his point of view, he retreated. He was quick to suggest that *his information might not have been the best* [italics mine]."

Finally, I have to wonder if Corso was not above playing a few cryptic mind-games with his readers, and even leaving a few snippets of clues for people to pick up on; clues which might have pointed in the direction of the human experiment angle of Roswell. For example, on allegedly seeing an alien body at Fort Riley in July 1947, Corso said: "At first I thought it was a dead child." We have seen that the matter of dead children crops up in relation to the Roswell-connected Project Sunshine, which utilized the remains of babies in their controversy-filled experiments. Corso also told his readers that he mused on the idea that the strange body came "from Hiroshima, [Japan]," or that it was "the result of a Nazi genetic experiment." Corso noted, too, that the alien had an "oversized incandescent lightbulb shaped head that looked like it was floating over *a balloon gondola* for a chin."

So in relation to the body which he claimed to have seen, we have Corso filling our minds with images of Hiroshima, Japan, Nazi experiments, a dead child, and...a balloon gondola. All of these issues are relevant to the book you have in front of you. Was this Corso's strangely warped and machinating way of trying to reveal obscure pieces of the puzzle, but without outright compromising the orders of whoever it was that secretly directed or encouraged him to write *The Day After Roswell*? Uncovering who, exactly, was steering Corso may one day lead us to the uncovering of the full dark story of Roswell itself.

Lt. Col. Philip Corso died on July 16, 1998 at the age of 83, approximately a year after his still-deeply-controversial book was published. His claims continue to divide the UFO research community twenty years after they first surfaced.

Philip J. Corso (second left), taken in Tokyo, Japan, 1953 (U.S. Army)

16:

A NEW SOURCE FROM DOWN UNDER

MONTHS after *Body Snatchers in the Desert* was published in June 2005, I received an out-of-the-blue email from a well-respected Australian UFO researcher, Keith Basterfield. As Keith notes of himself: "I have been interested in the subject of unidentified aerial phenomena (UAP) since the 1960's. Over the years I have held a variety of roles in numerous Australian state, national, and international organizations, studying the phenomena. My work has appeared in various state, national and international newsletters, magazine and journals. Between 2003 and 2008 I was involved in a search for Australian government documents relating to UAP with the Adelaide based AURA network."

Keith had a fascinating account to relate that dovetailed very closely with the data given to me by Al Barker, Bill Salter, the Black Widow, and the Colonel. Notably, the information was provided to Keith well before *Body Snatchers in the Desert* was published and when the existence of the book – and the story it told – was still firmly under wraps in the offices of Simon & Schuster in New York. It was after my book was published that Keith realized the data given to him some time earlier was eerily similar to that which I had uncovered. He wasted no time in getting in touch with me. I listened carefully to what Keith had to say.

* * * * * * * * * * *

A LONG-HELD SECRET IS FINALLY REVEALED

Tuesday, January 11, 2005, Keith told me, was the date on which he received a story just about as shocking and controversial as the ones I had uncovered between 2001 and 2003. On the day in question, Keith was interviewed on Australia's ABC 891AM radio station. The subject was the work of the Adelaide-based Australian UFO Research Association, in relation to the issue of so-called "UFO disclosure." Although Keith did not know it at the time, while he was taking part in the show, a caller phoned in, left his name and number, and asked for Keith to get in touch. He did precisely that.

It was later in the day that Keith made the call, in which his source somewhat hesitantly revealed snippets of a dark and dirty secret concerning certain things that went down – as in quite literally down – in the New Mexico desert in the summer of 1947. We're talking Roswell. Such was the potential dangerous nature of the information, Keith felt it was much wiser for the pair to meet up in-person, rather than discuss such matters over the phone. Keith was wise to follow his instincts; after all, one never knows who might be listening in.

When Keith related the account to me, he preferred not to use the informant's name and gave him an alias instead: Martin. Echoing this, Martin said to me that if I ever told his story, his name should never be revealed. It should be noted, however, that both Keith and I know Martin's real name. As Keith told me, he met Martin at the latter's home in Adelaide on January 15, 2005 – roughly six months before *Body Snatchers in the Desert* hit the bookshelves. The story went as follows...

* * * * * * * * * * *

FROM FATHER TO SON TO KEITH BASTERFIELD TO ME

Martin's father – a Brit – had worked for a certain arm of British intelligence decades before Keith got the story. I would later learn that the agency was MI5, which is the U.K.'s equivalent of the United States' FBI. Martin's father was sitting upon a secret of epic and grim proportions – one which he had *already* been silently keeping under wraps for years. Such were Martin's concerns and worries about sharing the story with Keith, he insisted that the information not be revealed to anyone – at all – without his, Martin's permission. Or, until after Martin's death, whichever came first. Keith agreed to the terms and sat back and listened as the dark and shocking tale came tumbling out.

Keith revealed that at the time Martin chose to share the secrets of his father, Martin's health was far from good. He was seriously ill – with a heart condition. It was possible that Martin was not long for this world, although he was not quite on his deathbed yet. The upshot was that Martin wanted to reveal to someone the story that his father had told him, while there was still time. Keith agreed to listen and also agreed not to place Martin's real, full name into the public domain.

According to Martin, he was told by his father of the truth of Roswell way back in 1959 – when Martin was only twelve years old. Such were his father's concerns about imparting what he knew, he asked young Martin never to reveal the story until he was either very old or on his deathbed. Given his serious heart problems that were in evidence in 2005, Martin thought it was a case of possibly now or never – hence his decision to share what he knew with Keith.

Martin's father had gotten all of the information on Roswell from a source working in the U.S. Intelligence community – who, exactly, we still don't know. Martin's father explained that the events which occurred out on the wilds of the Foster Ranch, Lincoln County, New Mexico in July 1947 were born out of early, and highly secret, experiments that had a bearing on the formative years of what would ultimately become the U.S. space program.

Keith, in a July 2011 online article, revealed what else Martin chose to share with him: "The Americans were working on getting into space. Their biggest concern was getting back to Earth and landing without killing the people inside the space vehicle. Landing in water was not considered, but a ground landing was the order of the day. The Americans were experimenting with craft they dropped from 'aircraft' flying in the stratosphere. Also, *gigantic balloons* [italics mine] were being flown in the stratosphere to drop craft fitted with retrorockets and a drogue chute. The retrorocket was fitted with an altimeter to fire them close to the ground. Lots of UFO sightings were of these craft. The U.S. released bogus flying saucer sightings and later discredited them."

Something that brings us squarely to Roswell.

* * * * * * * * * * *

"TWO TO THREE LIVE PEOPLE WERE NEEDED"

Martin recalled - to both Keith and I - how his father had informed him of a series of high-altitude experiments in the United States, in 1947, involving monkeys and pigs, in connection with the prototype aircraft / balloon flights. On *this* particular occasion, however – the one that spawned the ever-enduring legend of Roswell's crashed UFO – it was decided that a human crew was finally needed. Keith was told that "…Prisoners could volunteer for dangerous missions in return for early release but were not used in these experiments."

This issue of prisoners used in experiments, in relation to radical aircraft-based technology, is not a matter of doubt or a tale born out of folklore or conspiracy-theorizing. In 1948, staff of the Nuclear Energy for Propulsion of Aircraft (NEPA) program practically salivated at the idea of using prisoners in its aircraft-related trials. Official, now-declassified, records on this issue state: "The Committee is not in a position to make recommendations as to where these tests can be conducted other than that they should be carried out at some federal, state, or Armed Services prison, where life prisoners are incarcerated and where arrangements can be made with the prison authorities to cooperate in the experiment. The selection of the prison is a matter for top military consideration. *Continued cooperation of the prison staff and prisoners for a matter of many years will be required* [italics mine]."

That somewhat mirrored the words of my own informants in my 2005 book – namely, that prisoners were secretly offered reduced sentences if they were willing to engage in dicey and potentially missions for Uncle Sam. On this occasion, however, it was not prisoners who were on-board the ultimately ill-fated craft, but physically and mentally handicapped people. As Keith recalled: "Two to three live people were needed. The government got people with hydrocephalus - water on the brain - from a facility."

That, too, was something I had heard before, from the Black Widow, who learned of shocking human experimentation while working at the Oak Ridge, Tennessee-based atomic energy facility in the post-Second World War era. From the interview with Martin, both Keith and I recalled much more too on the matter of the human guinea-pigs. Keith said that the people roped in had "big heads, tiny bodies, jaundiced color - one even had no eyes. They put these people in the craft - either the balloon ruptured early or blew off course and came down. Retrorockets went off and set fire to it. It landed and a farmer / rancher saw it and reported it."

That "farmer / rancher," of course, was Mack Brazel; the man who let the Roswell cat out of the bag.

* * * * * * * * * * * *

A CERTAIN SYNDROME

As a quick aside, and on the matter of one of the people aboard the craft apparently having no eyes, this sounds very much like a condition called SOX2 Anophthalmia Syndrome. The U.S. National Library of Medicine describes SOX2 Anophthalmia Syndrome as "...a rare disorder characterized by abnormal development of the eyes and other parts of the body."

The NLM continues: "People with SOX2 anophthalmia syndrome are usually born without eyeballs (anophthalmia), although some individuals have small eyes (microphthalmia). The term anophthalmia is often used interchangeably with severe microphthalmia because individuals with no visible eyeballs typically have some remaining eye tissue. These eye problems can cause significant vision loss. While both eyes are usually affected in SOX2 anophthalmia syndrome, one eye may be more affected than the other."

There is also this from the NLM: "Individuals with SOX2 anophthalmia syndrome may also have seizures, brain abnormalities, slow growth, delayed development of motor skills (such as walking), and mild to severe learning disabilities. Some people with this condition are born with a blocked esophagus (esophageal atresia), which is often accompanied by an abnormal connection between the esophagus and the trachea (tracheoesophageal fistula). Genital abnormalities have been described in affected individuals, especially males. Male genital abnormalities include undescended testes (cryptorchidism) and an unusually small penis (micropenis)."

Taking into consideration the physical appearance of someone with SOX2 Anophthalmia Syndrome, it is hardly surprising that some of those who saw the bodies – civilians and military personnel alike – might have concluded the people were something more than human. And particularly so if some of those on-board had suffered from burns and / or catastrophic trauma from falling from the skies at high speed. Now, back to the story…

* * * * * * * * * * *

"THE EXPERIMENTS WERE CONDUCTED AT NIGHT"

According to what Martin said, one of the poor souls on-board the vehicle survived the crash. Not surprisingly, the military was determined to keep everything firmly under wraps. Even more so when, to their complete and utter consternation, the military learned that Brazel had reached the crash site first. He had even scooped up some of the materials that rained down on the ranch, such as portions of the huge balloon and the craft - and maybe even what was left of one or more of those people on board.

Martin had far more to say. He said that one of the big concerns the military had revolved around the possibility that some of the locals – including Brazel – might have found a few pieces of the shattered balloon and kept them as souvenirs, which is exactly what we are told *did* happen. Indeed, Brazel is said to have taken some of the wreckage to a small shed on the ranch property.

Briefly a storage area for the strange debris (Nick Redfern)

Martin additionally told Keith: "The balloons were of chrome-plated cellophane to reflect the heat. The experiments were conducted at night so balloons would not explode in the daylight."

This issue of the flight reportedly being undertaken at night is most intriguing. Although offered to Keith as a brief aside, it echoes the words of one of my sources – dubbed, in *Body Snatchers in the Desert*, as the Colonel. He told me that after the Roswell craft came crashing down to the ground, a retrieval team "searched the first night, sent aircraft up again, but it missed."

That, as the Colonel noted, a team of personnel was busily – and probably frantically – looking for the craft after darkness had fallen on New Mexico, is a good indication that, as Keith's informant advised him, this was indeed a nighttime flight. After all, if the test had been in the morning or even in the afternoon, then clearly the response would have been during the day.

It is worth noting too, the words of the U.S. Air Force when it suggested that a Mogul balloon was the culprit at Roswell. Like Martin, the USAF referred to regular balloons given a coating: "As early as May 1948, *polythene balloons coated or laminated with aluminum* [italics mine] were flown from Holloman AFB and the surrounding area. Beginning in August 1955, large numbers of these balloons were flown as targets in the development of radar guided air-to-air missiles. Various accounts of the 'Roswell Incident' often described thin, metal-like materials that when wadded into a ball returned to their original shape. These accounts are consistent with the properties of polythene balloons laminated with aluminum. These balloons were typically launched from points west of the White Sands Proving Ground, floated over the range as targets, and descended in the areas northeast of White Sands Proving Ground where the 'strange' materials were allegedly found."

* * * * * * * * * * *

"THE RANCHER TOLD EVERYONE IN TOWN"

Had Mack Brazel kept his mouth solidly shut about what he saw, the story of Roswell would possibly never have surfaced. Unfortunately for the military, Brazel most assuredly did *not* keep his mouth shut. Fortunately for us, he blabbed left, right and center – that is, until the crushing power of the government made him quickly clam up. And wise up, too.

The story is not quite over, however, as Keith confirms: "When I read Redfern's book and saw the similarities of the stories contained in this work with what Martin had told me, I told Martin of Redfern's research and conclusions. I asked that Martin release me from my commitment to remain silent. This he did in writing. Then with Martin's consent I told his story to Nick Redfern, who later interviewed Martin by phone from the USA."

* * * * * * * * * * *

"HUMAN-LIKE BUT STRANGELY DISFIGURED BODIES"

I did indeed interview Martin; in November 2005. He and I had a lengthy conversation on the phone late one evening, not long after Keith got permission to share the story with me. In some respects, Martin's account was different to the one provided to me in the early 2000s (handicapped people vs Japanese pilots), but both contained key and central issues - such as a human, rather than an alien, crew; the mention of a night flight, rather than one which occurred during the day; and the reference to both a test-craft and a large balloon array recovered at the scene.

This is not surprising, however, as all my original sources stated that six or seven such incidents occurred in broadly the same timeframe (give or take a month or so each way) and location, and ended catastrophically. The Colonel, for example, made it clear, that over the years certain aspects of these various events had weaved their way into a single unified story, that of Roswell: "This whole mess in the desert from May to August 1947 with the lifting-bodies and the high-altitude balloon programs – all of this has been rolled into one."

There was something else too: on several occasions during our phone call, Martin asked me if I thought his life might be in danger by revealing what he knew – and particularly so as a result of the information coming from his father who worked in British Intelligence. I said I doubted anything would happen to him as that would likely only legitimize his story and really make people sit up and listen. That he asked me three times if he might end up in trouble, however, made it clear to me that this issue was obviously playing on his mind to a near-torturous degree. Such is the level of fear that discussing the Foster Ranch event of 1947 can provoke – and decades later, even.

* * * * * * * * * * *

"HUMAN-LIKE BUT STRANGELY DISFIGURED BODIES"

One of the more intriguing things that came out during the course of our conversation was the fact that when, in 1993, the media reported on how New Mexico Congressman Steven Schiff was intent on uncovering the truth of Roswell, Martin penned a letter to the congressman's office, relating what he knew of Roswell from his father, back in 1959. Martin's letter has not surfaced (at least, not yet it hasn't...) from the correspondence collection that Schiff had with people who were involved in – or who were investigating – the Roswell controversy in the early 1990s.

I could not fail to note that 1993 was also the year in which the late CIA man and UFO researcher, Karl Pflock, aired his suspicions that Roswell might have involved the recovery of "human-like but strangely disfigured bodies" and which may have been linked to "*disclosures about the U.S. government radiation experiments* [italics mine] spawned in that same era."

It is a not widely known fact that Karl's wife – Mary Martinek - was Congressman Schiff's Chief of Staff. Was Karl exposed to Martin's eye-opening letter to Schiff? If the answer is a decisive "Yes!" then, time-wise, that might very well explain why Karl suspected for a while that there might have been a hidden and highly controversial military program at the heart of Roswell, rather than something of an extraterrestrial flavor. Karl was destined to change his mind, however, eventually becoming a champion of the theory that what came down was a Mogul balloon.

As for Martin, he was absolutely adamant that Roswell was a secret event of the early years of the Cold War. Aliens? Nowhere in sight. And certainly not on the Foster Ranch.

17:

A VANISHING BOOK AND SYNCHRONISTIC DATES

ALTHOUGH this particular chapter is focused on certain things that occurred in June 2005, I have to first inform you of something both strange and disturbing which happened in late 2004. It solidly sets the scene for what is to follow. Virtually all of the research was completed for *Body Snatchers in the Desert* by the end of 2003, and the first seven or eight months of 2004 were spent writing the manuscript for Simon & Schuster. Only days after I mailed a copy of the Word document to the publisher – yes, back then, publishing houses still wanted a paper copy as well an emailed attachment – it vanished, overnight, from the offices of S&S in New York. Josh Martino and Patrick Huyghe who both worked on the editing of the book, were perplexed – and more than a little disturbed and concerned too. Patrick, I recall, made a joke about it now being in the lowest-levels of the National Security Agency. He may not have been too wide of the mark.

My agent Lisa Hagan, however – who has been in the literary business for more than twenty years - was not at all surprised. It was, she said, practically par for the course when it comes to books on controversial subjects that might prove to be bad for your health. She told me:

> "If I want to do anything that is going to blow the whistle on something that the government doesn't want out

> there publicly, the government can shut that down – at the publishing house; they have people on the inside. It took me a long time after being rejected on certain projects to finally realize that what was happening to me was the same thing that had happened to my mother: Shut down by publishers on the stories the government didn't want out there.
>
> "I still work with these publishers – they do their job; I do my job. I do know that one of the publishers I worked with in New York – this was when all the manuscripts were printed – they had people who read the manuscripts *before* the editors got to them. I don't know which way it goes: Maybe, they were recruited by an agency when they were *already* working for the company. Or, they infiltrated it. But, I do know of people in the publishing industry who have been asked to be informants – asked by people in the government. There are definitely people who have been recruited."

And as someone whose books have made the front pages of *The New York Times*, *USA Today*, *The New York Times Book Review*, and *The Los Angeles Times*, Lisa should know.

* * * * * * * * * * * *

"THINGS GOT EVEN MORE SURREAL"

June 21, 2005 was the official publication date of *Body Snatchers in the Desert*. "Coincidentally," that was the very same day upon which a high-level meeting of a group known as the Nazi War

Criminal Records Interagency Working Group (IWG) was held at the National Archives in Maryland. In attendance were representatives of the CIA, FBI, Department of State, Department of Justice's Office of Special Investigations, National Security Council, and the Office of the Secretary of Defense. Some friends in the UFO research field privately suggested to me something weird. That the date issue was a deliberate action by shadowy individuals in the intelligence community who were engaged in some grand scheme; a scheme that was beyond the scope and full understanding of those outside of the Roswell loop.

The subject of the IWG meeting was notable: nothing less than a discussion to determine how many official files still existed on Japanese war crimes that were carried out during the Second World War. Much of the focus was on Unit 731 and its terrible, insanity-filled experiments. A large portion of all this was directed towards the extent to which the still-existing Unit 731 papers could be found and declassified.

It was, to be sure, a weird time: on the very same day that I began the publicity campaign to promote my book, certain, identical matters were being discussed by representatives of some of the most powerful and secret agencies in the United States. Things got even more surreal when, only one day later, I received a "Private Caller" phone call from a representative of the IWG. She expressed a great deal of interest in *Body Snatchers in the Desert*. I asked the woman how she knew of the book. In matter-of-fact style, she told me she had Googled "Unit 731" to see what was being said about the latest work of the IWG, and my book popped up – which made perfect sense, given the publication date of the book and the countless references within its pages to Unit 731. I outlined for her the Roswell story as it was told to me, she listened carefully, asked a few questions about names, sources, places and dates, and then thanked me and said her goodbyes.

There was, however, one somewhat strange aspect to the conversation. Just before hanging up, the woman casually announced that several of her colleagues had read my book *several weeks* earlier. This was, however, pretty much impossible, as the book didn't surface until June 21, only twenty-four hours before her call. Kindle wasn't introduced until November 2007 – so they could not have gotten a downloadable version of the book before the paperback hit the stands.

I found it very intriguing that she brought that matter up, almost in a baiting / goading fashion, knowing that I would be wondering how the IWG knew of the contents of the book before it had even surfaced. I did wonder if what her colleagues had access to was not the published book, but, instead, the Word document which went walkabout from Simon & Schuster's offices one mysterious night in 2004. If this was an attempt to try and destabilize me with strange mind-games, it was not going to work. And it didn't.

I did not hear from her, or from any other representatives of the IWG, again. It is, however, well-worth seeing what the IWG was saying on the very same day that my book was made available in Barnes & Noble, Borders (R.I.P.), and on Amazon.

* * * * * * * * * * *

"THESE DOCUMENTS WERE STILL HELD BY THE U.S. ARMY IN THE 1980S AND 1990S"

The IWG began as follows:

> "Chair Steven Garfinkel called the meeting of the IWG to order. He stated that thanks to the strenuous efforts of the three Public Members, Senator DeWine and Representative Maloney were able to extend the IWG through March 2007. The additional materials from the CIA make it likely that other IWG Agencies, especially FBI, DOD and State, will also have to review selected additional files during the period of the IWG extension.
>
> "Tom Baer reported that it was necessary that Senator DeWine and Representative Maloney held their February 2005 hearing to assure CIA compliance with the Disclosure Acts and extend the IWG. He noted that the previous Archivist had opposed the extension effort, but Allen Weinstein's support had been most welcome. Mr. Baer called the Chair's February statement a strong endorsement for the continuation of the IWG effort. Mr. Garfinkel added that he and the Public Members had met with the new Archivist on May 13, 2005, and he is most supportive of any effort to promote more access to information."

The minutes of the meeting reveal the following with respect to the CIA:

"Stan Moskowitz, CIA Director Goss's special representative for IWG matters, said that as a result of the February 2005 Congressional meeting, Mr. Goss has committed to declassify and release as much information as possible concerning Nazi and Japanese war criminals as the right thing to do. The release of two large files on Soviet double Agent Heinz Felfe is an indication of how serious the Agency takes its new commitment, according to Mr. Moskowitz. Mary Walsh reported that the CIA has already delivered more than 2000 new pages on Nazi war criminals and 3600 pages on Japanese war criminals. She expects to deliver more in July.

"Steven Garfinkel asked the IWG historians for their assessment of the new information from the CIA and whether the Agency appears in compliance with the Disclosure Acts. The historians unanimously replied that the new files transferred to NARA by the CIA were generally very informative, being more substantial and with fewer redactions. Richard Breitman said he has reviewed half the newly transferred files and that they are much more complete than previously. Messrs. Naftali and Wolfe noted that some questionable redactions remain.

"Norman Goda discussed the effort to create an additional name search list of non-Germans, based in part on extradition requests from the Hungarians and other East Europeans in the 1940s and 1950s. Mr. Shapiro said that the Holocaust Museum has received very good cooperation from the East European governments. In fact, he noted, the problem is how to manage the enormous new information that has been provided the Museum.

"Ms. Holtzman commented favorably on the CIA releases and the historians' positive assessment of the files. She wondered if there were enough resources available to continue this renewed effort.

"Mr. Rosenbaum stated that the IWG needs to develop a way to explain what they have and have not accomplished in the course of this work and how historians are in the best position to assess this. He also requested that as new name lists are created, OSI receive a copy. The remainder of the discussion of the CIA's presentation revolved around what the Final Report should say regarding what has and has not been accomplished."

Attention was then focused on the U.S. Army's files on Unit 731 and Japanese war crimes:

"Ms. Bromwell stated that a CD containing images of records related to Unit 731 that were deposited in the Library of Congress has been transferred to the IWG. She stated that no additional records from Ft. Detrick and the Dugway Proving Grounds have been located by the Army thus far. The issue of additional Army records related to biological experimentation noted in the book Factories of Death by historian Sheldon Harris remains open.

"Prof. Weinberg noted that the East Asia IWG volume will be a good forum for dealing with Dr. Harris' assertion that these documents were still held by the U.S. Army in the 1980s and 1990s."

In conclusion, there was the following: "Editor Kristi Rusch reported that volume of essays on Japanese war crimes-related records will likely be published in 2006.The publication must await the assessment of new records being transferred from the CIA.

> "IWG Information Officer Giuliana Bullard made a point of the media's interest in the newly-released CIA records as well as the NSA signals intelligence intercept summaries. She has drafted a plan for future announcements. During the discussion, the need for other IWG products, such as a glossary, was also noted. It was decided that when the two new CIA files on double agent Heinz Felfe are fully processed, they be the focus of a press release.
>
> "Mr. Taylor stated that the Historical Advisory Panel's fall meeting will review the chapter drafts of the IWG East Asian volume. The meeting was adjourned *sine die*."

18:

BODY SNATCHERS - THE UFO COMMUNITY'S REACTION

WHEN *Body Snatchers in the Desert* was published, I knew that UFOlogy would react with a mixture of skepticism, worry, anger and thinly-veiled hate. I was right – on all counts. Just before my book surfaced, Simon & Schuster unveiled the also-then-new book from good mate, Greg Bishop. Its title was *Project Beta* – an excellent book which was *also* focused on how the UFO issue has been used to hide military secrets. As luck would have it, I was in Greg's hometown of Los Angeles a few days after his supply of books arrived from Simon & Schuster. Greg signed a copy of his book for me with the following words: "Nick: Soon to be the most unpopular man in UFOlogy!" Greg proved to be quite the prophet. It wasn't down to psychic powers on Greg's part, however. Nope. Good old commonsense was all Greg needed. He knew exactly how UFOlogy would greet the book.

French researcher, Gildas Bourdais, who totally loathed the book, kept me active at *UFO Updates* for *months* with his persistent posts and comments. Not that that bothered me: I enjoy a good, online fight (ask Jason Colavito…). David Rudiak was overjoyed by the fact that by initializing the two first words of the book, he could forever refer to it as *B.S. in the Desert.* Karl Pflock was pissed that I mentioned in my book how, in 1993, he aired his suspicions that the Roswell bodies might have been linked to "disclosures about the U.S. government radiation experiments spawned in that same era." Why was Karl so put out? I never found out. I didn't care, either. Karl said it, so I quoted it. Things didn't end there.

There were a couple of researchers who said things that were downright libelous. I know this because a third-party who was CC'd on their emails was generous enough to forward those same emails on to me. One of the emails is framed in my office. It describes me as a "venomous troublemaker." I have to admit that phrase would have looked pretty cool written in white on a black t-shirt. And I even had one guy tell me he would never speak to me again because I was, and I quote, "full of fucking, steaming crap." Ah yes, UFOlogy at its absolute very best! Of course, the guy had to make his statement via the comfortable safety of the Internet. I prefer the face-to-face approach.

Then there was Kevin Randle.

* * * * * * * * * * *

"IF I COULD FIND EVIDENCE OF AN ILLEGAL EXPERIMENT"

Kevin and I disagree significantly on the matter of what the truth of Roswell really was / is. But, we are friends. We exchange emails now and again, Kevin has me on his radio show from time to time, and we had some interesting exchanges on the matter of the "Roswell Slides" fiasco that dominated much of UFOlogy of the last couple of years. We have hung out on a couple of occasions, too. And, I am pleased to say he has a fine sense of humor and, unlike certain researchers who will remain nameless, he can chat about things other than Roswell.

To his credit, Kevin did not let emotion get in the way when a constructive debate surfaced on the book and its revelations (I lack Kevin's ability to avoid exploding online – again, ask Jason Colavito). Kevin read the book carefully and gave his honest opinion on it, which I respected. In September 2005, Kevin wrote an article on my book for *Fate* magazine.

Interestingly, Kevin said, "...in fact, I have told many people that if I could find evidence of an illegal experiment that resulted in the deaths of human subjects, it would be a much bigger story, at least in terms of what the journalistic community would be willing to believe."

As Kevin also noted, though. "The problem for me was the lack of anything substantial."

He explained that he had carefully gone through various records from the likes of White Sands and the National Archives, but came up empty handed on the matter of controversial tests using humans. That didn't concern me though. You will now see why.

* * * * * * * * * * * *

"LITTLE INFORMATION IS AVAILABLE ON SPECIFIC EVENTS"

During the course of doing the research for my *Body Snatchers in the Desert* book, I spent a lot of time at the National Archives, Maryland, digging into files to determine what was going on at various New Mexico-based military installations during the summer of 1947. One of the files that I considered of potential interest - and which I still consider to be of potential interest - originated with Holloman Air Force Base, New Mexico and was titled "Holloman Air Force Base Range Safety, 1947-1959."

Prepared in 1960, it makes a number of intriguing statements:

> "The handling of range safety problems at the Air Force Missile Development Center, Holloman Air Force Base, New Mexico, has passed through three distinct phases. From the establishment of the Air Forces guided missile program at Holloman until the integration of the Holloman and White Sands Proving Ground test range in September 1952, Holloman was responsible for safety aspects of all its tests, including rocketsonde and balloon flights and research and development drone tests as well as missile tests in the narrow sense. Naturally there were many occasions for close coordination between the Air Forces at Holloman and the Army at White Sands on range safety criteria and procedures, for instance when the flight pattern of a missile took it over both of the adjoining test ranges."

Then, there was this statement: "*Little information is available on specific events* with regard to range safety during this period [italics mine]"

If, as this document demonstrates, by 1960 even Holloman's very own historians had "little" access to the history of the early years of research and safety issues at Holloman and its links with activities undertaken at White Sands (both in New Mexico.) then the idea that such a monumental story as the Roswell affair could remain successfully buried for decades seemed, to me, not so unusual after all.

* * * * * * * * * * * *

"IT HAS A NICE THEORY FOR THE TWO CRASH LOCATIONS"

There were a number of other issues that Kevin brought up. Here is one of them. In my book, I pointed out how the whistleblowers I spoke with between 2001 and 2004 told me there were two crash-sites on the Foster Ranch. And a third area from where a single body, but no wreckage at all, was secretly recovered – but not before its pummeled form was seen by four figures: Mack Brazel, Dee Proctor, Lewis Rickett and Sheridan Cavitt.

The reason why there were two sites is very simple: the device was comprised of a large balloon array and a craft, exactly as Martin's father had informed him. When a catastrophic event occurred in the sky, and the two detached from each other, the much heavier craft plummeted to the ground, while the far lighter, shattered balloon parts sailed down at a much lower rate of speed. And, of course, the collective trajectory of the balloon material was dictated by the direction of the wind. Hence there were two sites, some distance from each other, but still both on the ranch. Kevin admitted that such a scenario did make sense. He wrote: "Redfern's hypothesis does explain, to some extent, the various aspects of the Roswell case. It has a nice theory for the two crash locations; it explains why the government, in this case the military, would work so hard to hide the facts even today."

In my reply to Kevin – which was published in the same issue of *Fate* – I wrote: "Randle says that the book provides a 'nice theory' for the allegations that there was more than one crash site for the Roswell vehicle. It does. And we could argue the reason why the theory is so 'nice' is because it is the literal truth."

And, if two were not enough, there was a third site, too. Granted, what we know about this third site is steeped in speculation and innuendo, but that doesn't make it any less intriguing. It was in 1994 that Dee Proctor, who was involved in the case to a *still*-unclear degree when Brazel found the debris back in '47, drove his then-seriously-ill mother to a remote site on the Foster Ranch. It was approximately two and a half miles from the main debris site. In couched and enigmatic terms, Proctor told his mother that this particular site was where Brazel had found "something else."

What that "something else" actually was, is something that is very much open to speculation and opinion. Roswell researchers have suggested that Proctor was referring to a body. Maybe more than one. If so, perhaps this was the survivor that Martin told both me and Keith Basterfield about. Given that Proctor is now dead, the chances of us learning more on this "something else" comment are slim. This is most unfortunate, as a strong case can be made that Proctor knew exactly what occurred on the old Foster Ranch.

* * * * * * * * * * *

"A LOT OF PEOPLE ARE GOING TO BE DISTURBED BY THIS"

Certainly, the most glowing commentary on my book (almost the *only* one!) came from Stuart Miller. Before his tragic death in a traffic accident in 2011, Stuart (the editor of *UFO Review* and *Alien Worlds*) generated a great deal of positive publicity for the book, all of it in the face of much criticism from the UFO research community that hoped and prayed I was wrong. Stuart said:

"In *Body Snatchers*, Nick almost certainly offers the definitive explanation about what happened at Roswell. It may not be what you want to hear because I will tell you right now; it doesn't involve aliens, but as you read what he says, if your reaction is the same as mine was, then you will find yourself reluctantly coming to the conclusion that he has probably cracked it. As you read it, there is a 'dreaded' sense of feeling that it all just seems to make a horrible sense.

"There is a lot to take in and it will be difficult to absorb in one hit but as you do, you will be struck with a further wave of shock as you then consider the implications of what he has to say. They are very, very profound for this subject that we love. For others there will be a sense of relief that, as they see it, this albatross is finally removed from around their necks and UFOlogy can get on with its 'life' unfettered by the distraction of this incident."

Stuart continued, "the essential point of Nick's case is not new, although it actually may be new to you. The theory first surfaced with author John Keel about fifteen years ago, although he was off base quite a bit, but in the mid-90s *Popular Mechanics* got very close, indeed. Not quite there, but nearly. It is an interesting exercise to go back and read their piece again. They obviously had contacts.

"And others have been there too. It's been looked at, tossed around, laughed at, dismissed, and generally considered very unlikely. It will be a little harder to discard this time though. Nick presents new witness testimony and documentation and the way he pulls it all together

> is impressive. What is also interesting is the manner in which the story came to him. From two different separate strands, separated by five years. So the truth has been out there, of sorts, for a while. They have told us. They just didn't tell us they were telling us."

There was also this from Stuart:

> "There is bound to be controversy caused by Nick's conclusions and perhaps even mocking, and it would be naïve to expect otherwise. A lot of people are going to be disturbed by this. A lot of people have given their ufological professional lives to pursuing a particular aspect of Roswell or a particular case and all will be deeply affected and that should not be under estimated. The controversy will be welcomed. There are bound to be rough edges to Nick's story here and there and possible occasional inaccuracies, but it is unlikely they will undermine the core of his account. But Nick would welcome the interest and input of other researchers, without question. He hopes that people will go out and check up on what he has written for themselves, and possibly even take the story further. His narrative also opens up many other potential avenues of research.
>
> "If people accept what he has written and fully comprehend the consequences, then the affects will take time to filter through. The details, although a lot, you will take on board. It's the digestion process afterwards where the pain might come. Most of you though will be disappointed, but, we cannot hide from the truth."

* * * * * * * * * * *

"A DISTURBING BOOK"

Then there was Mac Tonnies, who offered the following:

> "The events at Roswell in the summer of 1947 -- dawn of the modern era of UFO sightings -- constitute a daunting mystery that has come to adopt the trappings of myth. While some evidence suggests a nonhuman presence in the New Mexico desert, alternative hypotheses abound. Nick Redfern's *Body Snatchers in the Desert*, a disturbing book that re-examines the case in light of the military secrecy prevalent at the time of the crash, posits that the supposed 'alien' bodies were in fact those of unwitting Japanese test subjects who perished in an aerospace mishap.
>
> "Although subjected to much criticism (mostly from within the UFO community), Redfern's hypothesis has yet to evaporate. Even if it ultimately fails to explain the eponymous 'Roswell incident,' it might lead to a broadened understanding of the military's role in the American Southwest at the beginning of the Cold War."

* * * * * * * * * * *

"IT SHOULDN'T MATTER IF THE 'GOOD OLD DAYS' OF UFOLOGY VANISH"

The final words of this chapter come from an interview undertaken with me by *Darklore's* Greg Taylor. I said to Greg that within UFOlogy there are a number of people who "...simply do not want Roswell to be anything other than alien, and whose blood-pressure sky-rockets when anyone dares to spoil their turf. It spoils the excitement and destroys belief systems, in other words. Too bad. Anyone whose Roswell conclusions are driven by emotion, plain belief, and an 'I want Roswell to be alien' approach, is way off course."

I added, "that is UFOlogy's biggest ever mistake: making Roswell a make-or-break case for the [UFO] subject. I actually don't think this has even been done consciously or deliberately, however. But the fact is there will be truly massive disillusionment within UFOlogy if Roswell falls. In fact, I do not even believe that the ETH [extra-terrestrial hypothesis] will survive within modern-day UFOlogy if Roswell falls - the stakes really are that high, in my opinion. But, so what? At the end of the day, it shouldn't matter if the 'good old days' of UFOlogy vanish. Getting the truth is all that should matter."

It's *still* all that matters.

19:

FROM ROSWELL TO LOCH NESS

AS someone who spends a great deal of time digging into stories of the distinctly strange kind, I find myself on the receiving end of a lot of correspondence from people that read my articles and books. Very often, people want to share their stories (or those of families and friends.) More often than not, this process opens a lot of doors and offers greater insight into the subjects that interest me – whether the UFO phenomenon, Cryptozoology, or the field of conspiracy-theorizing. Sometimes, however, I find myself on the receiving end of a very different category of story.

That category is, for me at least, quite possibly the most vexing one of all. The reason being that it is filled with intriguing stories, but ones that I have never been able to get to the bottom of, and which languish in a realm that might accurately be titled: "Fascinating but Frustrating." One such account has a bearing on the events at Roswell, Unit 731, and the worlds of psychological warfare and disinformation.

In 1997, as we have seen, the U.S. Air Force published a report that suggested the "alien bodies" seen sprawled around the Foster Ranch, Lincoln County, New Mexico in the summer of 1947 were dummies used in parachute experiments. They weren't. There is, however, another angle to the "alien dummies" saga, an incredibly odd angle.

* * * * * * * * * * *

"THE PLANNED USE OF PROPAGANDA AND OTHER PSYCHOLOGICAL ACTIONS"

Ten years after the Air Force's aforementioned report surfaced, I spoke with a man who claimed his grandfather, from the 1930s to the 1960s, worked in the world of Hollywood – in the field of special-effects and model-making for horror and sci-fi movies. The grandfather also had another string to his bow: namely, a connection to the secret world of government. And that same connection surfaced in an intriguing fashion.

In 1945, the acclaimed film-maker Billy Wilder – whose movies included *Some Like it Hot*, *Stalag 17*, and *The Seven Year Itch* and who died in 2002 at the age of 95 – directed the English language version of a documentary called *Death Mills*. It was a film produced by the U.S. Department of War's Psychological Warfare Department. *Death Mills* is a harrowing, but acclaimed, production that graphically revealed the sheer, horrific extent of the Nazi holocaust of the Second World War. The Pentagon describes psychological warfare as: "The planned use of propaganda and other psychological actions having the primary purpose of influencing the opinions, emotions, attitudes, and behavior of hostile foreign groups in such a way as to support the achievement of national objectives."

It transpired that plans were afoot for Wilder to make a similar production for the PWD. The subject? The atrocities undertaken by none other than Japan's Unit 731 during the Second World War. It was, however, a documentary that ultimately did not come to fruition. It transpires that my source's grandfather worked on *Death Mills* with Wilder and, as a result, came to know some of the

PWD personnel very well – as did Wilder, which is an important aspect of the story.

* * * * * * * * * * * *

FAKING E.T.

Almost certainly as a result of his work alongside the PWD on *Death Mills*, in 1955 the special-effects expert in question was contacted by psychological warfare planners in the U.S. Air Force and offered a lucrative contract: to use his cinematic skills to create what can best be described as faked alien bodies. Given the time-frame (namely, the mid-1950s), it would be wholly reasonable to expect that the Air Force would have wanted something to reflect the pop-culture of the day: the bug-eyed, Hollywood aliens of *This Island Earth* variety; the Krell of *Forbidden Planet*; or the "Martian mutants" of *Invaders from Mars*. But not so.

The man was asked to design and create eight "alien bodies." There was just one proviso: they all had to be very life-like, dwarf-ish, hairless, and topped off with huge heads. Reportedly, so the grandson told me, his grandfather was paid very handsomely for approximately three months of work, which was undertaken in a specially modified trio of rooms at a military base "in southern California."

It doesn't take a genius to guess that the man asked why on earth the Air Force wanted him to fabricate a number of extraterrestrial corpses. He could understand the military taking an interest – and a very deep interest – in *real* alien bodies, but faked ones constructed by a Hollywood special-effects expert? What was the point? Well, the point, it seems, was a fascinating one.

"Scuttlebutt" and rumor that reached the man's attention suggested a fantastic operation was at work. In fact, it was an operation that was two-fold in nature. First, there was a bizarre plan for the military to photograph the "bodies," strategically laid out on gurneys or slabs, and then have the images sent anonymously to the Russian Embassy in Washington, D.C. Along with the photos would be a long and winding fabricated letter – one supposedly written by a communist sympathizer in the U.S. military - warning the Soviets that the U.S. Government had got its hands on alien bodies and technology and was well on its way to perfecting that same technology. The latter issue echoes the Philip Corso saga, which surfaced in 1997 in *The Day after Roswell*, and which also revolved around claims concerning the secret back-engineering of alien technology.

* * * * * * * * * * *

DESPERATELY SEEKING IVAN

It was a strange example of Cold War-era psychological-warfare proportions; an example designed to scare the hell out of the Russians and have them waste their time chasing down what were really non-existent aliens. There was, however, a second part to the story.

There were suspicions, at the time, that at Wright-Patterson Air Force Base, Dayton, Ohio, several employees were selling secrets to the Soviets, particularly secrets born out of the work of Wright-Pat's Foreign Technology Division (FTD.) So, a plan was formulated: carefully expose those same commie-loving characters to a couple of "alien bodies," strategically placed in a vault or bunker, and have them believe Uncle Sam has recovered a crashed UFO, or several, along with their deceased crews.

Then, it was a case of keeping an eagle-eye on all of those under suspicion and see which of them – if any, of course – might be prompted to do something out of the ordinary, such as make a phone call to a man named Ivan, or meet in a local park with a trench-coat-wearing character with a foreign-looking appearance. It was a program designed to ferret out Soviet sympathizers in the military by exposing them to a huge secret that, in reality, was a huge ruse.

While it all sounds rather bizarre, if you think about it carefully, it also makes a lot of sense. After all, what better way to mess with the Soviet mind – and to root out dastardly Reds in the United States – than by (a) dangling a fabricated carrot, and (b) reeling in the enemy without any real secrets ever being compromised?

If true, this saga may very well help to explain some of the controversial stories where military personnel have reportedly been exposed to alleged alien bodies in underground rooms (such as the "Hangar 18" legends attached to Wright-Patterson Air Force Base) and under "convenient" circumstances that many skeptical researchers think are just too good to be true. They just might be. But not for the reasons that the skeptics think.

The reason? The eyewitnesses may have been set-up as a test of their loyalties. It may have been intended all along for them to see the "bodies" (or, more correctly, the dummies). If they kept quiet about what they saw, they were good soldiers and trustworthy. If they told their wives or girlfriends, they were potential security risks and perhaps needed to be watched carefully in future. And if they ran to a Soviet handler, it was jail-time.

This, of course, leaves us with a pair of highly thought

-provoking questions: if the story told above is one hundred percent accurate, does that mean *all* the stories of "alien bodies in the morgue" are born out of this long-gone Cold War operation / deception? Or, does the government have real extraterrestrial corpses on ice, and, if so, is it using the "dummy" angle just to confuse things even more?

* * * * * * * * * * *

ALIENS AT ROSWELL? NOT "NESSIE-SSARILY"

One final thing for you to contemplate on, something which takes us back to Billy Wilder, to Unit 731, and to Roswell, too. They are all issues which Wilder almost certainly knew a great deal about, as amazing as that might sound.

In 1970, Wilder's *The Private Life of Sherlock Holmes* was released. In the movie, the British Government constructs a small and revolutionary submarine which is secretly tested in the deep waters of Loch Ness, Scotland. In the event that the submarine might be seen by members of the public, by the media, or – worse still – by pre-First World War German spies, the Brits attach a Nessie-style head and neck to the submarine. The result is that people think they are seeing the legendary monster, rather than a secret craft of Britain's Royal Navy. One more thing: the submarine is so small that it is manned by a family of brothers who previously worked in a circus. All of them are dwarfs. In one particular scene, two of the brothers are killed during a secret test in the loch.

Consider this: some of the secret experiments undertaken in New Mexico in the summer of 1947 involved people of short stature, some of whom died. The experiments were hidden behind a mass of faked UFO tales. In Billy Wilder's *The Private Life of Sherlock Holmes* dwarfs are also used in highly-classified, military experiments. Those experiments, too, are hidden behind tales of a strange enigma. In this case, it's the Loch Ness Monster. And some of the submarine crew die. Now, take note of the following…

The truth of the Roswell affair was successfully hidden by experts in the domain of psychological warfare. In 1945, Billy Wilder worked *very* closely with psychological warfare agents of the U.S. military while producing *Death Mills*. Wilder was also briefed by Army psychological warfare experts on the work and history of the Roswell-connected Unit 731 – for a documentary that was ultimately never made. All of this strongly suggests Wilder (a) kept in touch with his PWD buddies after the filming was complete, (b) at some point post-July 1947, learned at least some of the truth of Roswell and the Unit 731 connection, and (c) was inspired by that secret knowledge to create a highly entertaining movie. It was a movie which replaced a UFO with a lake-monster, and replaced dwarfish handicapped people with dwarfish circus employees, but which left the basic template – of classified military experiments, of dwarfs, and of curious cover-stories of a paranormal nature - intact.

So we have one man who made alien models in the 1950s to fool the Soviets, and (in a fictional setting) we have a government creating a monster to fool the Germans. There is a Billy Wilder tie to both issues, in the sense that the primary individual in the E.T. "dummy" saga actually worked with Wilder on *Death Mills*. Somewhere in this convoluted saga, there is a big secret just waiting to be uncovered. It surely will, pardon the pun, only get wilder.

20:

AREA 51 AND SOVIET MUTANTS

IN yet another intriguing twist in the seemingly never-ending saga that goes by the name of "Roswell," a further theory for what happened on the Foster Ranch surfaced in 2011. In some respects, at least, it mirrored certain portions of data contained in my *Body Snatchers in the Desert* book, which is the one – and the *only* - reason I make mention of it here. That theory appeared in the pages of Annie Jacobsen's book, *Area 51: An Uncensored History of America's Top Secret Military Base.* The book included a very strange story suggesting that the Roswell craft and bodies were, in reality, the diabolical creations of a pact between the notorious Dr. Josef Mengele - Nazi, SS officer, and deranged "Angel of Death" - and Soviet premier, Joseph Stalin. It was a story told to Jacobsen by an elderly man named Alfred O'Donnell; a man who had links to none other than Area 51.

In May 2011, UFO investigator Tony Bragalia, who outed O'Donnell, stated: "Ms. Jacobsen's source about this Roswell story is unnamed by her in the blockbuster book. He wanted to remain anonymous. Annie Jacobsen kept her promise. I did not learn her source from her or from anyone associated with her publishing company. His identity and his background is revealed here and now."

Bragalia continued: "Alfred O'Donnell is nearly 89 years old and he is one of Annie Jacobsen's key sources about this Roswell crash story 'interpretation.' O'Donnell is indeed exactly who he claims to have been. In the early 1950's he was at the "Nevada Test Site" where atomic bombs were tested regularly. O'Donnell was indeed part of the nucleus of top management and engineers for EG&G - one of our nation's top defense contractors. Founded as Edgerton, Germeshausen and Grier (EG&G) the company was acquired by URS Corporation some years ago. URS employs over 50,000 and is the leading designer and builder of federal classified facilities in the United States. They work with military as well as with the Intelligence Community (particularly the NSA) in constructing and operating some of our nation's most sensitive and secret facilities."

Bragalia made his position clear: he concluded that O'Donnell truthfully related the story as it was told to him, decades earlier. But Bragalia also believed that O'Donnell was lied to and fed disinformation to further muddy the Roswell waters.

* * * * * * * * * * *

"DID ANYONE EVER NOTICE THAT THE NAZIS AND STALIN WERE ENEMIES?"

The purpose of this early Cold War plan was, said Jacobsen, to plunge the United States into a kind of *War of the Worlds*-style panic (echoing the infamous Orson Welles radio-broadcast affair of 1938) by trying to convince the U.S. Government that aliens were invading. And how would the plan work? By placing grossly deformed children (courtesy of the crazed Mengele) inside a futuristic-looking aircraft designed by the brilliant aviation experts, the Horten brothers, and then fly the craft to the United States and try and convince the American people of the alien origins of both.

Unfortunately for Stalin, the plot failed when a storm brought down the craft and its crew in the wilds of New Mexico, an event that did not lead to widespread panic, but that instead was hastily covered-up by U.S. military authorities.

Was the story true? Was Jacobsen duped? Was the whole thing a blend of fact and fiction, weaved by government insiders to *even further* confuse the true nature of what did, or did not, happen outside of Roswell back in the summer of 1947? Whatever the answer, I found it intriguing that several central themes of the story divulged to Jacobsen paralleled some of the data provided to me for use in my *Body Snatchers in the Desert* book back in 2005.

On the matter of the unlikely nature of the story, it is well worth noting that the Horten aircraft were not radio-controlled. This raises an important point: how could mutated German children fly an aircraft across Europe and the Atlantic and land it in the United States? Such a scenario is manifestly absurd. Note the words, too, of Kevin Randle, who rightly questioned the wisdom of the Russians utilizing a Horten craft to deceive the U.S. Government. As Kevin correctly noted: "...the Air Force had access to the Horten Brothers designs after the collapse of Nazi Germany and should have recognized the craft if that is what it was." Kevin also offered two questions which Jacobsen has not replied to: "Did anyone ever notice that the Nazis and Stalin were enemies? Did anyone notice that Mengele had fled to South America and was no longer any sort of important person in 1947?"

Kevin's questions are as valid today as they were when this saga erupted in 2011.

Josef Mengele, the "Angel of Death" (Public domain)

* * * * * * * * * * * *

THE HORTEN ANGLE

Although my book chiefly focused on alleged diabolical human-experimentation undertaken by the Japanese during - and shortly after - the Second World War by its beyond-notorious Unit 731, it did focus to a significant degree on two issues that are central to the data that was provided to Jacobsen, as I'll now demonstrate.

We'll start with the Horten brothers. As my 2005 book revealed, two of the old-timers from U.S. Intelligence I interviewed *did* say that at least two of the aircraft that were test-flown at White Sands in 1947 and led to the legend of the Roswell incident, were based upon the revolutionary aircraft designs of the Horten brothers, Reimer and Walter.

Second, one of my informants said of the Roswell bodies that, "...there was no doubt that they were human - handicapped humans - and from Japan or China, I would say to you. Some were obviously the result of inbreeding and some showed characteristics of larger heads, some what I now know to be Progeria, six fingers; all kinds of syndromes."

Progeria is chiefly a condition that affects children - the reason being that those affected by Progeria simply do not (for the most part) reach adulthood, as a result of the ways in which it ravages the human body. Progeria also causes the person to exhibit certain symptoms: a dwarf-like body, an enlarged head, and a lack of hair - all reportedly characteristics of the Roswell crew.

So, yes, there may well have been a Horten connection to Roswell – and there is little doubt that physically handicapped people were used in the 1947-era experiments? But, piloted across the Atlantic from Russia? Not a chance in hell. Or even in Roswell.

* * * * * * * * * * *

FACT VS FICTION: THE FLYING SAUCER

There is also the weird saga of a man named Bernard Newman that, to a degree, echoes the Stalin / Mengele angle - namely to create a staged, alien event to influence and provoke government concern and response. Published in Britain in June 1948, Bernard Newman's novel, *The Flying Saucer*, was the first in the world to deal with the emotive topic of crashed flying saucers. The book tells the tale of an elite group of scientists that decide to "stage" a series of faked flying saucer crashes, with the express purpose of attempting to unite the world against a deadly foe that, in reality, does not exist.

The Flying Saucer begins with a series of worldwide "UFO crashes" (involving distinctly terrestrial vehicles built for this task): the first in England, the second in New Mexico, and the third in Russia. The "crash sites" are carefully chosen and involve all of the three major powers that emerged out of the carnage of the Second World War. But, the work of the scientists is only just beginning. Not content with creating its bogus UFO crashes, the team takes things one step further and constructs a faked "alien body" that is pulverized in one of the crashes, and is then presented to the world's scientific community as evidence of the alien origin of the creatures that pilot the craft. As a result of these events - and with remarkable speed - the many and varied differences between the governments of the Earth dissolve under the "Martian" threat and the final chapter of Newman's book sees practically every international political problem hastily resolved.

So, we have a story told to me (between 2001 and 2004, and published in 2005 in *Body Snatchers in the Desert*), and a story provided to Annie Jacobsen and published in 2011.

Yes, of course, there were big differences: in Jacobsen's book the Roswell event is the result of a failed Soviet, Cold War-era deception, and in my book the incident results from the equal failure of a secret, domestic operation. Weird-looking aircraft designed and built by the Horten brothers, handicapped children with large heads and dwarfish bodies, and faked UFO events: key components of two stories told to two authors, and both linked with Roswell.

Are we seeing evidence of governmental deception, perhaps of a definitively psychological warfare nature? Is one story true and the other a mutated, distorted version of the truth, but spread and carefully altered by disinformation artists at an official level to confuse the Roswell saga even more? Here is where things get even more mystery-filled.

* * * * * * * * * * *

A "VERY CURIOUS AND CONVOLUTED MIND GAME"

The angle of insiders with links to Area 51 being told that Roswell was a Soviet hoax (and involving genetically-altered human beings) is an intriguing one. Now, just so there can be no misunderstanding, I don't mean that because it's intriguing I believe it's the answer to the puzzle. I certainly don't. It's intriguing to me because the scenario of Area 51-linked people being told such a story did not begin with Jacobsen's informant, Alfred O'Donnell, at all. Six-months *before* Jacobsen's book was published, my book, *The NASA Conspiracies*, was released and included a whole chapter that told the tale of a man who had worked at Area 51 in the early 1970s, and who had heard a very similar story to that told to Jacobsen. In fact, it was near-identical.

It's a strange and convoluted saga involving a man named John who, while working out at Area 51, was exposed to a series of weird and controversial files that told astonishing tales of alien visitation and UFO crashes in the early, formative years of the flying saucer era. As I note in *The NASA Conspiracies*:

> "John stressed that although the documentation at issue certainly looked genuine, he was never able to entirely dismiss from his mind the possibility that his exposure to the files could have been a part of some large and very curious and convoluted mind game on the part of NASA and the intelligence services, such as the CIA, Air Force Intelligence, and the National Security Agency. John speculated that his bosses may have exposed him to totally bogus materials at Area 51, and then watched his every move to see if he spoke out of turn, and to those without security clearances. The fact that John never did speak out of turn in that twelve month period, and was thereafter considered utterly trustworthy, led him to be rewarded with a near decade long career in the private security sector. It was a career that saw him move, practically effortlessly, within highly influential circles in the world of U.S. Intelligence that were totally unconnected to UFOs."

To me, at least, this was all very refreshing. Whistleblowers are generally extremely keen to have their story believed; but John noted to me from the absolute outset that the nature of the data to which he was exposed should be addressed very carefully, and not accepted uncritically at all. And there is more. John related an aspect of the story to me that was published in my NASA book, and which dealt with one set of papers he read that, today, we can see is highly relevant to the account provided to Jacobsen. I described it in the pages of my 2010 book like this:

> "...John did assert that there was a brief collection of documents dating from July 1947 speculating that this might have all been the result of *a very ingenious hoax on the part of the Soviets* [italics mine] - until, that is, it very quickly became acutely apparent to one and all that not even the Soviet Union would have had the required expertise to successfully pull off such a fantastic ruse, much less biologically alter, or mutate, a number of human beings into something very different."

To me, this was important, as we have old files (that ultimately found their way to Area 51 - they did not originate there) discussing the two central points of the story later told to Jacobsen: (a) the idea that Roswell was a Soviet ruse; and (b) the theory that the bodies found at the crash-site might have been biologically altered or mutated by the Russians. The story told by John, and published by me in late-2010, is *astonishingly* close to the one provided to Jacobsen months later. The big difference, of course, is that Jacobsen's Area 51 source believed the Russian theory, while John, also of Area 51, was highly suspicious of it and practically dismissive of it.

But, that such files did apparently exist at Area 51, and did refer to both the Russian hoax angle and the issue of genetically altering human beings, does make me think that this Russian-themed story / theory was indeed in circulation among Area 51 personnel at some point decades ago. And, maybe, some of the employees who were exposed to the files, to the rumors, and (as John speculated as a possibility) to some weird loyalty-testing mind-game, came to accept the Russian story as being utterly genuine; when in reality the truth was very different.

And things are still not over.

* * * * * * * * * * *

"AN ELABORATE AND WELL- ORCHESTRATED HOAX (MAYBE BY THE RUSSIANS)"

The next part of the story comes via the notorious "leaked" MJ12 documents – MJ12 supposedly being a highly classified group within the U.S. Government that handled the most sensitive parts of the UFO issue, and as far back as 1947. I'm not talking about the original documents that first publicly surfaced in Tim Good's May 1987 book, *Above Top Secret*, and that shortly afterwards surfaced just about here, there and everywhere. Rather, I'm talking about the even more controversial collection that came to researchers Dr. Robert Wood and Ryan Wood via UFO researcher Timothy Cooper in the mid-to-late-1990s – a man who you became acquainted with in an earlier chapter.

There seem to be four prevailing theories regarding the Cooper documents: (a) they are the real thing (extremely unlikely); (b) they are government disinformation (highly likely); (c) they are the work of someone in the public UFO arena acting alone, and who - by creating the documents - was intent on helping to champion Roswell as an alien event (interesting and plausible); and (d) they were still the work of someone within UFOlogy, but who was getting the data for inclusion in the documents from old-timers who wanted to spill the beans, but in a fashion that would not come back and haunt them and provoke a government-driven backlash (not at all impossible).

Of the documents that Cooper had in his possession, one is a highly-controversial paper titled "Interplanetary Phenomenon Unit Summary" of 1947. As you might guess by its title and date, the IPU summary describes the events that have come to be known collectively as the Roswell incident. It provides names, dates, places and events that tell an extraordinary story - and it's a story that some support, many dismiss as outright fabrication, and even more have forgotten, two decades after the files surfaced.

There is one very intriguing entry in the document. It appears in the last-but-one paragraph of the IPU report, and is presented as, essentially, the tentative conclusions of officialdom regarding what did, or did not, come down outside of Roswell in 1947. It states: "Our assessment of this investigation rests on two assumptions: 1) Either this discovery was an elaborate and well-orchestrated hoax (maybe by the Russians), or; 2) Our country has played host to beings from another planet."

As I mentioned in an earlier chapter, the Cooper collection of material is as intriguing as it is controversial. But, I did find it very thought-provoking that (regardless of who wrote or created the documents, and for whatever purpose - obscure or otherwise) the IPU document suggested that U.S. authorities had allegedly addressed the idea that the Roswell event was borne out of a "well- orchestrated hoax (maybe by the Russians)."

This is, of course all very relevant to the story told to Annie Jacobsen and cited in her *Area 51* book. Did her source, Alfred O'Donnell, see the IPU document at some point decades ago? Did he have access to further files (or testimony) relative to how this determination of a Russian hoax was made? What was it that prompted the creator of the IPU document to include that particular data on the "Russian hoax" in its pages? Are the MJ12-Cooper files nothing more than fabrications by UFOlogists with far too much time on their hands? Or is the revelation above indicative of something weirder going on, such as a disinformation-themed plot to confuse the truth of Roswell?

Whatever the answer, the fact is that there is *yet another* disputed document that addresses the Russian hoax / mass hysteria angle. The story can be found in what is known as the "White Hot Technical Report." The 19-pages-long document (real, disinformation or hoax - one is forced to take one's pick) states in part: "There is a good chance that the Russians may try to make use of the flying saucer scare by public news media and diplomatic means of a technological breakthrough in aircraft and missile development. We feel that such a disclosure would most certainly cause great embarrassment to our elected officials and to the military, not to mention the panic felt by the citizenry."

* * * * * * * * * * *

"DR. MENGELE EXPERIMENTED ON THE FAMILY"

Finally, one of the reasons why a very small number of UFO researchers felt there might be some truth to the story as told to Annie Jacobsen by Alfred O'Donnell was because Josef Mengele actually *did* have a twisted and very disturbing interest in dwarves and children. As evidence of this, one and all should take a look at Yehuda Koren's book, *Giants: The Dwarfs of Auschwitz*, which is an eye-opening read, to say the very least.

The press-release for Koren's book said:

> "*Giants: The Dwarfs of Auschwitz* is a moving and inspirational story of survival, of a troupe of seven dwarf siblings, whose story starts like a fairy tale, before moving into the darkest moments of their history; the darkest moments of modern history. At a time when the phrase 'survival

> of the fittest' was paramount, the Ovitz family, seven of whose ten members were dwarfs, less than three feet tall, defied the fate of so many other Holocaust victims...
>
> "...Descending from the cattle train into the death camp of Auschwitz, the Ovitz family was separated from other Jewish victims on the orders of one Dr. Joseph Mengele. Obsessed with eugenics, Dr. Mengele experimented on the family, aiming to discover the biological and pathological causes of the birth of dwarfs. Like a single-minded scientist, he guarded his human lab-rats, and subsequently, when the Russian army liberated Auschwitz, all members of the family - the youngest, a baby boy just 18 months-old, the oldest, a 58 year-old woman - were alive."

Whatever the truth behind the recollections of Alfred O'Donnell, one thing we can say for sure is that a great deal of effort went into carefully creating a scenario revolving around Josef Mengele, Joseph Stalin, the Horten brothers, mutated children, and Roswell. The MJ12 documents that surfaced in the 1990s addressed the same "Russian hoax" controversy. I published the story in 2010 – thanks to my source, John. Half a year later, Annie Jacobsen, in her *Area 51* book, revealed an almost identical account. Someone – even to almost this very day, it seems – is still intent on obfuscating the truth of what took place at Roswell with bogus tales and files that are likely examples of well-thought-out disinformation, but with a degree of genuine data thrown into the mix, just to confuse things even more. The truth is out there? Yes, it is. But, whose truth is the *real* truth?

21:

A TREASURE-TROVE OF FILES

THE late Kathy Kasten was a feisty and outspoken contributor to the now-defunct online discussion forum, *UFO Updates* (her articles included "How I Decided to Become a Loud-Mouthed Woman"). She was also a good friend of mine; I enjoyed, and could relate to, her never-ending piss-and-vinegar approach to UFOlogy. Much of Kathy's research was focused on the ever-controversial Roswell affair of July 1947, a subject which had fascinated her since the 1980s. And, as Kathy's investigations progressed, she found herself looking more and more into a certain installation in New Mexico that, she came to believe, was directly connected to the Roswell enigma. Its name: Fort Stanton. Yes, the very same Fort Stanton that has popped up previously with regard to (a) people with extreme physical handicaps and (b) Japanese balloons.

On August 7, 2012, Kathy died from a cardiac arrest. As far back as 2005, I had been corresponding with her on matters relative to Roswell and her suspicions that the incident had *nothing* to do with aliens, but *everything* to do with post-war experiments on human guinea-pigs. At the time of her death, Kathy was working on a full-length book on her theory – parts of which closely matched the findings I detailed in *Body Snatchers in the Desert*, which was encouraging.

So far as I am aware, no serious attempt was made by Kathy to find a publisher. She wanted to have the entire manuscript completed before submitting it to a publishing house rather than just hand over a brief synopsis and a sample chapter or two. Time and fate, however, stepped in and prevented the next step from coming to fruition. Perhaps realizing that she was on a time-limit, one which was closing in, in early 2012 Kathy surprised me by emailing me to say that she was planning on handing over copies of her Roswell files to me, in the event that I might want to make use of the material – any of it or all of it - should I ever decide to write a sequel to my 2005 book.

* * * * * * * * * * *

A MOUNTAIN IN THE MAIL

It was shortly after Kathy died that her family got in touch, as they had decided to donate to me all of Kathy's research files, correspondence, and much more – and not just her Roswell-based material. Which was, of course, extremely generous of them. A week or so later, a large amount of files turned up on the doorstep, collectively contained in heavy cardboard boxes. To say there were thousands upon thousands of pages of material, dating back decades, would not be an exaggeration. An Aladdin's cave? Pretty damn close, to be sure.

Due to work and what is known as life, it took me several months to go through the entire collection, some of which had nothing to do with Roswell in particular - and nothing to do with UFOs in general, either. Probably a full third of the material was focused on issues relative to mind-control and mind-manipulation, such as the CIA's notorious MKUltra program of the 1950s. And there was a lot of material on post-Second World War files on unethical experiments on people in the 1940s and 1950s – which certainly *was* linked and relevant to Roswell. There was also a great deal of correspondence between Kathy and various UFOlogists (including certain *very well-known* Roswell researchers), which made for illuminating and, at times, highly amusing, reading – for libelous reasons that those same researchers probably would not want publicizing. Maybe one day though. You know: just for the fun of it…

* * * * * * * * * * *

ON THE TRAIL OF "RANDY" LOVELACE

I'll get to Kathy's Fort Stanton research in the following chapter, but I'll begin with her investigations into the life, career, and potential Roswell connections, of a man with an intriguing history. Kathy's notes and records show that from the early 1990s to the mid-2000s, she spoke with a few interesting characters, of a somewhat shadowy nature. They advised her that if she wanted to uncover the truth of Roswell, she would be wise to pursue the work and history of a certain William Randolph "Randy" Lovelace II.

That Kathy's dossier on Lovelace is about five-inches thick demonstrates that she carefully followed the advice of her sources and left pretty much no stone unturned when it came to the matter of exploring a possible Roswell-Lovelace connection. Of course, for those who aren't aware of the man himself, there is a big question that needs answering: who, exactly, was William Randolph Lovelace II? Well, let's take a look.

* * * * * * * * * * *

"A PROMINENT AMERICAN SCIENTIST"

To say that Lovelace was a fascinating character is an understatement. Born in 1907, he was a physician who graduated from Harvard Medical School in 1934, and, in 1938, took up a position with the Aeromedical Field Laboratory at Wright Field, Ohio (today, Wright-Patterson Air Force Base). It was at Wright Field that Lovelace undertook groundbreaking research to understand how exposure to high-altitudes could affect the human body and nervous system. Experiments with new and novel oxygen masks and parachutes were of paramount importance, too.

A colonel with the Army Air Corps in the Second World War, Lovelace was awarded the Distinguished Flying Cross and – in 1947 – helped to establish the Lovelace Foundation for Medical Education and Research, in Albuquerque, New Mexico. Then, in the late 1950s, NASA invited Lovelace to chair its Special Advisory Committee on Life Sciences.

Such were his skills in aviation medicine, Lovelace worked closely alongside the original NASA Mercury astronauts. Then, in 1964, Lovelace was appointed to the position of NASA's Director of Space Medicine. The Lovelace Crater on the surface of the Moon is named in honor of the man himself. There was, however, a more secretive side to Lovelace, a side which linked Lovelace to nothing less than the Paperclip operation, to the CIA, and to national security issues, as investigative writer Hank. P Albarelli, Jr., notes:

William R. Lovelace II, a Roswell player (Public domain)

"Dr. Ulrich Cameron Lutz [was] hired through Project Paperclip in 1947 to perform rapid decompression experiments at SAM [the School of Aviation Medicine at Brooks Air Force Base, San Antonio, Texas]. From 1951 to about 1963, Lutz served intermittently as a consultant on high altitude acclimatization for both the Air

> Force and the CIA...In 1954, William Randolph Lovelace II, a prominent American scientist who maintained a long-standing relationship with the CIA, invited Lutz to head the Department of Physiology at the Lovelace Clinic for Medical Education and Research in New Mexico. The CIA's Project Oxcart made extensive use of the Lovelace Clinic in the training of high altitude spy pilots."

William Randolph Lovelace died as a result of a plane crash in December 1965, in Aspen, Colorado. Both his wife and the pilot were killed, too.

* * * * * * * * * * *

LOVELACE AND ROSWELL

Kathy's files suggest there was another side to Lovelace – nothing less than a highly-classified connection to the analysis and study of the Roswell crew; or, at least, of one of them. It's important to note that Lovelace's name has popped up several times in relation to Roswell. Kathy, then, was not alone in making the link. For example, when *Body Snatchers in the Desert* was published, in 2005, Stan Friedman wrote: "Of particular importance is that Nick never mentions William Randolph Lovelace who was head of aviation biology for Wright field during World War II. Afterwards he was on their Aviation Biology Committee while back running the Lovelace clinic. He even jumped out of an airplane at 42,000 feet to determine how soon one should open one's parachute without freezing to death on the way down. He and his family had founded the Lovelace Clinic in Albuquerque to be kind of the Mayo Clinic of the Southwest. They had many government contracts to evaluate animals such as sheep which had been exposed to radiation. They did a lot of classified work for the government. I believe that they would have done some initial evaluation of the bodies found near the crash on the Brazel ranch and in the Plains. They had the competence, were close by, and had the security clearances."

True, I didn't mention Lovelace in my book. The reason was very simple, though: back then, I had no data linking him to the events on the Foster Ranch, at all. So, why on Earth would I mention him? But, others have made a connection in far more recent years. In 2016, Tom Carey and Don Schmitt said: "As a result of Lovelace's proximity to Roswell and his medical expertise, we had long heard rumors of his being involved in the incident. Then, in 2011, we had the good fortune to meet with neurosurgeon Dr. Mark D. Erasmus of the Presbyterian Medical Clinic of Albuquerque, who informed is that years before he had worked with a nurse who worked with Lovelace back in 1947."

That nurse was a woman named June Crain, who was in the employ of the military at Wright-Patterson from the early 1940s to 1953. Crain stated that Lovelace was indeed sent to Roswell on a secret mission, adding that he would say very little upon his return to the base, aside from admitting that he had been in Roswell and making a vague reference to "a new species."

Now, let's take a look at what Kathy Kasten learned from the Roswell-Lovelace link.

* * * * * * * * * * *

"MANY HEALTHY INDIVIDUALS SUBMITTED TO AN ARRAY OF TORTURES"

Kathy wrote in her notes for her planned book: "Lovelace had been in Germany in 1939 on a Mayo Clinic fellowship, learning new surgical techniques, visiting various facilities and checking out equipment, and looking at the leading edge in aviation medicine. Lovelace had spent time with the infamous Hubertus Strughold, looking into the German research that was done using low pressure chambers. Although, detainees in various German concentration camps had been used as 'test subjects' in the pressure chambers. Strughold – who oversaw the programs – claimed he knew nothing.

> "Strughold came to America and 'fathered' aviation medicine. However, after his death his name was taken off the Hubertus Strughold Aeromedical Library at Brooks Air Force Base and Ohio State University erased Strughold's likeness from a stain glass window. Therefore, we can say that Lovelace collected the research from projects based on a lack of regard as to whether the subject lived, died or was permanently disabled. More than that, the detainees were coerced into participating. They had no choice but to participate."

The Project Mercury astronaut Wally Schirra had nothing particularly positive to say about Lovelace and his work. Kathy quoted Schirra's words in her dossier on Lovelace; a quote that would have eventually become, one assumes, part of a chapter in her book.

Schirra stated that the many and various tests undertaken on him and his colleagues at the Lovelace Institute amounted to "... an embarrassment, a degrading experience. I have said many times – and meant it – that it was a case of sick doctors working on well patients. I make the point in talks to medical associations. It was a rarer, almost unheard of situation in which so many healthy individuals submitted to an array of tortures – proctoscopies, barium-enhanced x-rays, psychological interrogation and so on. The doctors at Lovelace were trying to establish a physiological and psychological baseline to use in tests during a space flight. Much as I'd rather not knock a dead man, Randy Lovelace did a lousy job."

Now, we come to the important part.

* * * * * * * * * * *

LEADS START TO DEVELOP

Under the terms of the Freedom of Information Act, Kathy secured various file on Lovelace. They provide a great deal of material on the man and his work on human-subjects – in terms of both aviation and space-flight. While a number of names are blacked-out in the files – as often happens when files are declassified – others are not. Kathy made a list of all those names, as well as the names of as many people she could find who knew Lovelace, who worked with him, and who met him. And, if they were still alive, Kathy tracked them down and spoke to them – almost exclusively by telephone, as Kathy's abundant notes on this issue make very clear. It was an incredible and laborious task that, to a degree, paid off.

When the question of a Lovelace-Roswell connection surfaced, nearly all the people Kathy spoke with claimed no knowledge of such a connection. Three refused to speak with Kathy on such matters, which is likely to be of no significance in the slightest. After all, most people probably *would* put the phone down if a complete stranger called them up and started asking questions concerning the Roswell UFO affair. But, Kathy did have her breakthroughs. One such breakthrough concerned what became known as the Women in Space Program – a project to which Lovelace was directly tied.

* * * * * * * * * * *

"THE LOVELACE DOCTORS REQUIRED VERY THOROUGH EXAMINATIONS"

The New Mexico Museum of Space History notes that Lovelace assisted NASA in terms of profiling "...the perfect astronaut, based on years of medical testing experience of pilots. These guidelines were used to help select astronauts for the Gemini and Apollo programs. Lovelace believed that these guidelines showed that women were just as capable of space travel as men, and in 1960, he helped chose 25 female astronaut candidates, some of which were selected as the 'Mercury Thirteen' the next year. The program was abruptly cancelled however, in September 1961."

There is a good reason why I mention the female astronaut program. Read on.

NASA says of Lovelace's work in this area: "Lovelace's Woman in Space Program was a short-lived, privately-funded project testing women pilots for astronaut fitness in the early 1960s. Although nothing concrete resulted, the women who participated have since been recognized as trailblazers, whose ambitions to fly the newest and the fastest craft led them to be among the first American women to gain access to sophisticated aerospace medical tests."

* * * * * * * * * * * *

SECRETS IN THE CEMETERY

Kathy had a notable breakthrough when it came to the issue of Roswell, Lovelace and the Woman in Space Program. It came in 1994. Frustratingly, the source of the account is listed in Kathy's papers only as "Danni." It must be said at this stage that, at times, Kathy got quite paranoid about her Roswell research and its implications, which probably explains why she was so careful not to place too much information on her sources in her extensive files. That, on a couple of occasions, certain files of Kathy's were stolen, makes her approach understandable.

In fact, in her final years Kathy told me of how she believed she was being followed, that her phone was monitored, and that her mail had been tampered with. She also told me she had received several menacing and threatening phone calls, as a result of her Roswell / Lovelace research. You can find the details of many of Kathy's run-ins with government-types in my 2015 book, *Men in Black* – which includes lengthy statements from Kathy on such matters and which collectively run to fourteen pages. It may be for those specific reasons, and combined with an understandable degree of paranoia, that Kathy elected to hold back from placing all of her findings on her hard-drive. Or even in print. And that includes information on Danni. Now, back to the story.

When, in 1980, the Berlitz-Moore book, *The Roswell Incident*, was published, Danni's mother told her a strange story; the implication being that with Roswell now in the public domain, it seemed okay to talk about things a bit more. At the time, Danni was in her late teens. The *original* source of the story, Kathy discovered, was a woman who joined Lovelace's astronaut program, and who was a cousin to Danni's mother. Under circumstances that Danni did not wish to reveal to Kathy, her relative told the family a strange story concerning Lovelace's involvement in the inspection of a "deformed man" held at "an Army hospital in New Mexico" in the late 1940s. The man was short in stature, had an oversized head, and was severely mentally handicapped. Not only that, the man was the solitary survivor of the crash of some kind of "airplane" which had come down relatively close by.

Danni - who, in 1994, was then thirty-two - was well aware of the Roswell story, and told Kathy that the man had suffered a number of injuries, that he was "picked up at the ranch" (a reference, almost certainly, to the Foster Ranch) – and was rushed by military personnel to the aforementioned "Army hospital." It quickly became clear to Kathy that the installation Danni was describing was none other than Fort Stanton, which is *very* close to the Foster Ranch. As for the other members of the crew, given that they were all dead when the military got to the crash-site, their remains were hastily taken to "the Roswell base and preserved," as Danni worded it.

According to the dark, family secret, Lovelace was brought in to assess certain aspects of the man's injuries, such as major damage to his spine and neck. A detailed report was prepared by Lovelace for the military. Reportedly, the man died less than a week later. Incredibly, Danni's family heard that the body of the curious-looking man was quickly buried in Fort Stanton's huge cemetery. And when I say huge, I mean it. The official website of Fort Stanton states: "Selected for its healthful climate, [Fort Stanton] served some 5,000 sailor patients between 1899 and 1953, *1,500 of whom are buried in the Maritime Cemetery on a hillside overlooking the Fort* [italics mine]."

Interestingly, researcher Martin Cannon says: "'Coincidentally' or otherwise, the Brazel ranch is located quite near Fort Stanton Mesa, an old military outpost commanded by Kit Carson during the Indian wars. By the time of the Spanish-American War, this facility was converted to use as an army hospital. During World War II, soldiers suffering from combat fatigue and other psychological ailments were remanded here. Researcher Kathy Kasten visited Fort Stanton Mesa and toured the facility's cemetery. *She noted with great interest the sharp increase in deaths in the 1947-51 period* [italics mine]."

22:

SHE "FORT" THE LORE

THE origins of Fort Stanton date back to the middle part of the 19th century. Its purpose was purely strategic: The fort – named after one Captain Henry W. Stanton who was killed in battle in 1855 - was constructed to act as a place from where military personnel could take on the forces of the Native American Mescalero Apache people. To this day, the latter still live in south-central New Mexico. Notable characters who spent time at Fort Stanton included the famous frontiersman, Kit Carson, and the infamous outlaw, Billy the Kid. To ensure that it could withstand assaults from the local tribe, Fort Stanton was constructed out of stone, rather than timber, which was very often used in the construction of military forts at the time.

The hostilities between the Native American people of the area and the military presence at Fort Stanton provoked decades of antagonism, confrontations, and even more combat. It was not until the latter part of the 19th century that matters finally calmed down. That was when the Mescalero Apache people were provided with a reservation and Fort Stanton closed its doors. At least, for a few years. Just one year before the dawning of the 20th century, however, the base was reopened. Fort Stanton's new role was very different, however: it became a hospital, one designed to take care of patients with tuberculosis. It did so well into the early 1950s, having treated more than 4,000 patients, more than 1,000 of whom died and who are buried in the fort's cemetery.

Although Fort Stanton continued to take good care of tuberculosis patients during the Second World War, at the height of the hostilities with the Nazis, Italians, and Japanese military, it became a detention center for what were then termed "enemy aliens." The list included more than thirty Germans – from a liner, the *S.S. Columbus*, which had been rendered useless by the British military, near New York City, in 1939 - and a dozen and a half Japanese. The official website of Fort Stanton notes that the facility, in the early part of the war, served as a "refuge for a group of Japanese-American families threatened by mobs in their hometowns."

Eight years after the end of the Second World War, the facility's staff again refocused their work on people afflicted by tuberculosis. That is, until the 1960s – which is when it became known as "The State Hospital for the Developmentally Handicapped." Since then, it has acted as a place that has treated those with alcohol and drug issues. In 2007, Congress officially made Fort Stanton a National Conservation Area.

All of which brings us back to Kathy Kasten.

* * * * * * * * * * * *

"AMERICAN-JAPANESE EX-INTERNEES FROM A NEW MEXICO SECRET DETENTION CAMP"

In Kathy's files, in 2013, I found something interesting written in a notepad – and which she had later turned into a Word document. It read: "My research has uncovered the fact that the American Government was testing many different types of aircraft at the time of the Roswell crash; some of it for the purpose of forming the basis for a future space program, and perhaps even one that involved American-Japanese ex-internees from a New Mexico detention camp."

Particularly notable is the fact that the date of the original note was March 23, 1992. This was, of course, long before the Japanese / secret experiment angle of Roswell was on the radar of almost no one in UFOlogy. Certainly, my *Body Snatchers in the Desert* would not be published for another thirteen years. We now know, however, that as far back as the 1990s, Kathy was pursuing a near-identical angle to the one I was exposed to in the 2000s.

Whether you agree with Kathy's thesis or not, there can be no doubt whatsoever that the "New Mexico detention camp" to which she referred in 1992 was Fort Stanton. Now, let's take a very close look at what Kathy uncovered about a Roswell-Fort Stanton connection. We'll also see what she concluded about that very same connection.

* * * * * * * * * * *

SEEKING THE TRUTH

In 1992, Kathy circulated to a number of friends and colleagues in UFOlogy – those with an interest in the Roswell affair – a document she had prepared and which outlined her hypothesis:

> "Based on my field research in 1992 in the State of New Mexico, the information now being presented to the general public is in fact just another layer down, more disinformation, of the cover-up of whatever happened in New Mexico in July of 1947. Because I am not a UFO investigator per se, but rather an empirical data

collector, I do not feel bound by what is now considered the traditional approach to the event. I am governed by research rules which require that facts / evidence be presented in a way that is verifiable by any and all persons of goodwill who wish to discover the truth of what is being stated."

It's important to note that Kathy, up until the latter months of 1991, was quite open-minded on the possibility that Roswell was an alien event. That stance changed – radically so – in early 1992, as we saw with regard to her March 23, 1992 notes cited above. So, what was it that made her change her opinion to a significant degree? The answer is very strange and paranormally-tinged.

* * * * * * * * * * *

WELCOME TO THE WORLD OF THE "SILENT PARTNERS"

Kathy wrote that in the winter of 1991...

"...I began to be approached on a subtle level by a group of entities who apparently do not reside in the same space / time continuum I do. At least, this is how I explained it to myself. After a number of contacts, we formulated an agreement in the form of an equal partnership. I suppose, you would need to call them my Silent Partners. By an equal partnership, I mean a free and open exchange of information. Naturally, as an empirical data collector, I listened to their information and agreed to keep an open mind. I conveyed to them

> that I would neither accept nor reject their data until I tested it. I regarded the experience as an experiment, and I was participating as an informed research subject." Kathy then went on to describe the members of the team:
>
> "The information they, two separate teams – two men formed one team, and a single woman the other, communicated to me by a combination of imagery and symbolic language...The woman – short and dark-haired – started the contacts in December of 1991. The information I received from her was in the form of photograph-like images..."

Kathy continued:

> "In addition to the information I received from the Silent Partners, I worked with a pendulum suspended over a map of New Mexico. Working with a pendulum is a time-honored method sometimes utilized even by archaeologists, but not always admitted to publicly. The pendulum picked up two places on the map, an area just east of the Gallinas Mountains and an area off a man east / west highway, State 380. Just after these areas were located, in an altered state, I could see myself moving along a deeply rutted dirt road bordered on both sides by a barbed-wire fence on top of a mesa. Immediately after this scene, I came upon a very sharp jog in a dirt road and a water tower was located just ahead on my right.
>
> "I felt I had received enough information to locate whatever it was that I was being impelled to find. One

> of the questions I asked during an altered state session was 'Why now?' The answer came back, 'Because it's enough. It's just enough of this being hidden."

The location that Kathy had picked up on, and was describing, was Fort Stanton.

A portion of Fort Stanton, New Mexico (Public domain)

* * * * * * * * * * * *

"I WOULD NOT HAVE REALIZED JUST HOW STRANGE THIS WHOLE SAGA REALLY WAS"

Kathy's files reflect that certain figures within the Roswell research community were highly skeptical of the possibility that Kathy was receiving data on the case from her so-called "Silent Partners" and from "...a group of entities who apparently do not reside in the same space/time continuum."

In addition to that, a friend in that same Roswell research

community provided Kathy with copies of letters from a variety of UFO researchers who, in 1992, were making tasteless jokes about Kathy "hearing voices" in her head. This was not the case at all, however. Kathy was a very intelligent person and she astutely knew that any references to her receiving information from mysterious, psychic sources was bound to provoke controversy on a large scale. So she kept her cards very close at hand. There was an extremely good reason for this.

While Kathy's words about strange men and women who did not "reside in the same space/time continuum" implied to some that her sources were, themselves, aliens, that's actually not so. Had I not received Kathy's correspondence and files in 2012, and dug into it all to a very deep degree in 2013, I would not have realized just how strange this whole saga really was.

* * * * * * * * * * *

PSYCHICALLY SPYING

On occasion, Kathy led certain Roswell researchers to believe that her sources were something more than human, chiefly to keep them away from something even more intriguing; something *she* wanted to solve and take the credit for. In that sense, she was buying time, provoking diversions, and wanting to be the person who solved Roswell. Admittedly, there has been a great deal of laughable, ego-driven rivalry in the Roswell research community – and for decades. It is primarily driven by the desire to be "the first with the most." For so many, it's not just about solving the case, it's about who gets to the finishing line quickest.

As for Kathy's sources, they certainly spent time in what

could be called a very different "space / time continuum." But, they weren't aliens. They were remote-viewers. For those who may not know what remote-viewing is, I refer you to IRVA, the International Remote Viewing Association. The group states:

> "Remote viewing is a mental faculty that allows a perceiver (a 'viewer') to describe or give details about a target that is inaccessible to normal senses due to distance, time, or shielding. For example, a viewer might be asked to describe a location on the other side of the world, which he or she has never visited; or a viewer might describe an event that happened long ago; or describe an object sealed in a container or locked in a room; or perhaps even describe a person or an activity; all without being told anything about the target - not even its name or designation."

* * * * * * * * * * *

SECRETS OF THE CAPITOL BUILDING

For years, the U.S. Intelligence community and the military utilized highly skilled remote-viewers to psychically spy on the likes of the former Soviet Union, China and Iran – among many others. In 1991, however, a U.S. Army team of remote-viewers was tasked with trying to get to the bottom of the Roswell affair. This is where things get downright mysterious. According to Kathy's notes, the Army's remote-viewers were responding to a hushed request from certain figures in the United States Capitol – better known as the Capitol Building – to figure out what the hell happened back in

'47. Those in the Capitol who had heard whispers of the Roswell affair chose to quietly ask certain powerful figures what were undeniably probing questions. Asking such questions resulted in responses along the lines of: "Don't get involved in things that don't concern you."

To two of the people in the Capitol Building, this hostile response was like a red rag to a bull. As a result, a certain small group within the military was given the order to remote-view the Roswell saga, the crash-site, and the surrounding areas – all under clandestine circumstances, of course. How did Kathy know all this? Let's see.

* * * * * * * * * * *

"IT BEGAN AND ENDED AT FORT STANTON"

When I first introduced you to Kathy and revealed that, after her death, her files were given to me, I said: "Probably a full third of the material was focused on issues relative to mind-control and mind-manipulation, such as the CIA's notorious MKUltra program of the 1950s."

There is a reason why I mentioned that. We come to it now.

As well as investigating aspects of the UFO phenomenon, Kathy was deeply pursuing ongoing research into the field of how the human mind could be controlled and manipulated. The large amount of material in her files shows she was mixing with, and talking to, a *lot* of people with military and intelligence-based backgrounds. And they weren't all retired. We're talking, primarily, about the period from 1989 to 1994. Those same sources were not only working on mind-control programs for the Department of

Defense, but were also looking to take the remote-viewing programs of the 1970s and 1980s to entirely new levels.

It was from those DoD-connected contacts that Kathy learned an arm of the military was readying itself to secretly remote-view Roswell. As a direct outgrowth of this suggestion, word went up "the chain of command" to the point where wheels were put into motion and the operation to crack the mystery of Roswell via psychic means began. All of which got back to Kathy via her "Silent Partners" in the project.

It was just a few weeks into the program that Kathy was visited by several members of the team, the people whose real identities she carefully obfuscated. Yes they had incredible skills. Yes they negotiated strange unearthly psychic realms - and just about as easy as most of us negotiate a highway or a subway. But, they were as human as you and me; just a bit more finely tuned when it came to the scope and power of the human mind. Kathy's records show that, according to the results of the Army's quest for the truth of Roswell, and in Kathy's own handwritten words, "It began and ended at Fort Stanton."

* * * * * * * * * * *

DANNI: MORE THAN SHE APPEARED TO BE?

While she was still in touch with her insider sources – contacts which abruptly ended in 1995, and for reasons which are not even alluded to in her records – Kathy learned something notable. That the RV results described a scenario involving several people secretly transferred from Fort Stanton to Alamogordo, who were then used in a high-altitude exposure-based experiment in early July 1947, and who lost their lives in the process. That is, aside from one of the crew, who survived the crash, for a while, at least. That was the man who was hastily and secretly taken back to Fort Stanton where attempts were made to save his life. It was all in vain: the man soon died and his body was quickly disposed of, on-site, in the fort's cemetery.

The above, of course, sounds very much like the account of Danni – Kathy's informant who told her an almost identical story, and also in the 1990s. In fact, so incredibly similar was Danni's story to that provided to Kathy by her remote-viewing contacts, I have to wonder if we aren't missing sizeable pieces of a very large jigsaw. I have mused several times on the possibility that Danni's involvement in all of this may have been more complex than Kathy ever realized. Kathy's records show that, in her opinion, the surfacing of Danni and her story was the result of fortuitous good luck and nothing else. I cannot dismiss, however, the possibility that Danni may have been some kind of plant, someone *seemingly* innocent and with a "family secret" to tell. But, someone who, in reality, may well have been part of the remote-viewing program; someone subtly pushing Kathy even further in the direction of Fort Stanton. True or not, from thereon Kathy turned most of her attentions in the direction of that old 19th century fort.

* * * * * * * * * * *

"A LARGE MILITARY RESERVATION LOCATED VERY CLOSE TO THE FOSTER RANCH EVENT"

In May 1992 Kathy made her first trip of a handful to Fort Stanton. Amusingly, at one point Kathy gave serious consideration to trying to find the body of the man who lost his life and engage in a bit of grave-robbing. Or, at least, grave-investigating. Kathy's lawyer quickly nixed that idea, however. In her notes on her various excursions to Fort Stanton, Kathy wrote, in May 1992, something that shows where her thoughts were at long before most people in UFOlogy dared to address the human angle of Roswell:

> "The reason I found myself walking the fields of Fort Stanton Mesa came about because I was bothered by the possibility that the so-called Roswell Incident had been the result of covert testing. There were all kinds of experiments taking place just after World War II. America was determined to become a world power. My reasoning / intuitive inkling for anything involving the Fort Stanton Mesa area had to do with the fact that it was a large military reservation located very close to the Foster Ranch event. There is a great deal of reservation acreage that acts as a buffer zone. I wondered if research project managers had thought the same thing. Little did I know at the time that parts of the Fort Stanton military reservation had served as a camp for the incarceration of Japanese-Americans claimed to be 'troublemakers.'"

In the concluding section of her never-published manuscript on Roswell, and on her investigation of the Fort Stanton angle, Kathy wrote that the purpose of her script was to "...open discussion and change the nature of inquiry regarding the various crashes that took place in and around Lincoln County, New Mexico in the late-1940s. Real events did take place and various agencies did participate in covering up the true nature of those events."

Kathy added that her planned book "...does not suggest

those events had anything to do with the crash of an extraterrestrial vehicle. By accident or design, a way to cover real events was discovered by agencies who wanted to hide covert research projects from the American public. The UFO cover story could be put out by an agency on the one hand, only to be denied on the other hand. Creating a circle of information that could/can easily be controlled. That is the real story of the Roswell Incident."

It's interesting that Kathy referred to "the various crashes," rather than just one. That accords with what all of the sources referenced in *Body Snatchers in the Desert* said, that there were multiple events in New Mexico in the summer of 1947.

* * * * * * * * * * *

THE BACKBONE OF ROSWELL

While Kathy's story is one worthy of a big-bucks spy-thriller of the kind that Hollywood moguls love, it is not a tale of fiction. In fact, there are certain aspects of her overall saga that dovetail nicely with what else we know about Roswell. For example, and as I noted in the previous chapter of this book, according to the revelations of Danni, "Randy" Lovelace was brought in to assess certain aspects of the injuries of the Roswell survivor, such as major damage to his spine and neck.

Tom Carey and Don Schmitt note that one of those who examined the Roswell bodies was a Dr. Lejeune Foster, who the pair describe as "a renowned expert and authority on human spinal-cord structure." Reportedly Foster – who had worked with the FBI during the Second World War - examined the bodies somewhere in Washington, D.C. Although Carey and Schmitt place the

Dr. Foster story strictly in the context of dead aliens, it's worth noting that Foster's role was to "check their bone structure, spinal cords, and vertebrae..."

This sounds not at all unlike the story of Randy Lovelace having been brought into Fort Stanton to check out the damage to the spine of the solitary survivor. Interestingly, Dr. Foster, too, told of a single survivor of the crash. Like so many who were involved in the Roswell affair, Foster was fearful of saying too much to anyone.

* * * * * * * * * * * *

"FUNDS WERE BEING SPENT WITHOUT APPROPRIATE OVERSIGHT TO MAINTAIN A FALSE STORY"

Then there is the matter of the Capitol Building and Roswell, as described in relation to Kathy Kasten's experiences in the early 1990s. It just so happens that the Capitol Building and Roswell also surface in yet *another* story, that of the late Jesse Marcel, Jr., the son of Major Jesse Marcel, who was present at the crash-site in July 1947. According to Marcel, Jr., in the early 1990s he received an invite to meet with a "mysterious government official" in none other than the aforementioned Capitol Building. The meeting went ahead. The subject: the Foster Ranch events of 1947. Marcel, Jr. said of that same official figure:

> "He told me that he had been charged with the responsibility of investigating the operation of a 'black government' within the government, where funds were being spent without appropriate oversight to maintain a false

> story about the Roswell incident and cover the true story up. He said that his job was to report to the Senate Appropriate Committee, and advise them as to where these dollars were going, and why."

Was it down to mere chance that both Jesse Marcel, Jr., and Kathy Kasten found themselves plunged into the seemingly separate worlds of Roswell and the Capitol Building? No it surely was not. And as we can say with a high degree of probability, those two worlds weren't quite so separate, after all.

Of one thing we can be sure: in the early 1990s certain figures in the world of government – and operating out of the Capitol Building – were looking to unravel Roswell, once and for all. Part of that investigation involved government people speaking with those who saw the Roswell wreckage - such as Jesse Marcel, Jr. Then, there were those who were proactively pursuing the remote-viewing angle: a small group tied to the U.S. Army which focused heavily on Fort Stanton.

And caught up in the bizarre and conspiracy-filled maelstrom was Kathy Kasten.

* * * * * * * * * * *

ALIENS VS. ENEMY ALIENS

One final thing to muse upon with regard to the Kathy Kasten-Fort Stanton issue: it's worth noting that, during the Second World War, those who were suspected of being hostile to the United States, such as Japanese and Germans living within the U.S., were typically referred to as potential "enemy aliens."

Wikipedia describes the term as follows: "In customary international law, an enemy alien is any native, citizen, denizen or subject of any foreign nation or government with which a domestic nation or government is in conflict with and who are liable to be apprehended, restrained, secured and removed. Usually, but not always, the countries are in a state of declared war."

Indeed, during the Second World War, the U.S. Government created the Alien Enemy Control Program (AECP). Staff at the National Archives note: "Immediately after the bombing of Pearl Harbor, President Roosevelt issued Presidential Proclamations 2525, 2526, and 2527 to authorize the United States to detain allegedly potentially dangerous enemy aliens. The FBI and other law enforcement agencies arrested thousands of suspected enemy aliens, mostly individuals of German, Italian, or Japanese ancestry, living throughout the United States."

The National Archives' staff add: "By the end of the war, over 31,000 suspected enemy aliens and their families, including a few Jewish refugees from Nazi Germany, had been interned at Immigration and Naturalization Services (INS) internment camps and military facilities throughout the United States. Some of these internment locations included Sharp Park Detention Station, California; Kooskia Internment Camp, Idaho; Fort Missoula Internment Camp, Montana; Fort Stanton Internment Camp and Santa Fe Internment Camp in New Mexico; Ellis Island Detention Station, New York; Fort Lincoln Internment Camp, North Dakota; Fort Forrest, Tennessee; and Crystal City Internment Camp, Kenedy Detention Station, and Seagoville Detention Station in Texas."

As a result of the creation of the AECP, the term "alien" quickly became well-used in 1940s-era America – but *not* in the way that so many use that same term in the 21st century.

Today, people so often equate the word "alien" with something of an extraterrestrial nature and origin. If, however, even just a handful of stories flew around Roswell and the surrounding areas in the summer of 1947 - in which the term "enemy alien," or even just "alien," was used to describe recovered Japanese bodies - it's not at all implausible that, decades later, memories of the word "aliens" would take on a whole new meaning in some quarters, *an out of this world meaning.*

Imagine an old soldier, on his death-bed and taking his final breaths. He struggles to reveal to his family the day, as a young man, he helped to secretly recover the bodies of aliens from the wilds of New Mexico. Perhaps he really meant creatures from a faraway star-system. On the other hand, maybe he was trying to reveal hidden truths of another kind of alien: an alien that was once seen as the enemy kind.

23:

"THE VICTIMS OF THE WRECK"

ONE of the most intriguing pieces of Roswell-based documentation is that which has become known as the "Ramey Memo." It is a single piece of paper and can be seen in a black-and-white photograph taken of Brigadier General Roger Ramey. In 1947, he was the head of the 8th Army Air Force which operated out of Fort Worth, Texas. Ramey is a key part of the story, as he is holding the memo in question in his left hand; a memo which says something about Roswell. But what? That's the issue UFO researchers are unable to agree upon. The controversy over what the memo shows began years ago, but it gained far more momentum in the 2015-2016 period.

What we know for sure is that the photo was taken at Fort Worth on July 8, 1947 by a man named J. Bond Johnson. At the time, he worked for the *Fort Worth Star-Telegram* newspaper. What we also know is that as researcher Barry Greenwood notes, an entire series of pictures was taken by Johnson "in response to an AAF press release that the debris recovered from the alleged Roswell UFO crash was a weather balloon. The debris itself was displayed in an office for Johnson to photograph which he did and his pictures were widely distributed the next day in national newspapers."

What we *don't* know for sure, though, is what the memo says. At least, not completely.

* * * * * * * * * * *

"THE PHOTOS WERE OF INSUFFICIENT QUALITY"

Yes the memo can certainly be seen in the photo, with the text pointing outwards, albeit in slightly folded fashion. A number of attempts have been made to decipher the memo. The first real attempt of any major significance was undertaken on behalf of the U.S. Air Force. In their massive 1995 report on the Roswell affair, the USAF stated that it sent the photo-collection to what was only referred to as a "national-level organization for digitizing and subsequent photo interpretation and analysis." The results, however, were disappointing, as that same unnamed organization informed the Air Force, on July 20, 1994, that even after careful digitizing, "the photos were of insufficient quality to visualize either of the details sought for analysis."

It's interesting to note that, to this very day, the Air Force refuses to identify the aforementioned "national-level organization." On top of that, Air Force states that the relevant documentation generated by the organization cannot now be found.

As we have seen on several occasions, missing files are a staple part of the Roswell case.

* * * * * * * * * * *

"THERE ARE VARIOUS KEYWORDS AND PHRASES THAT CAN BE READILY SEEN"

With the turning of a new century, UFOlogy undertook its very own attempts to solve the mystery of the Ramey Memo and what exactly it says. One of those was UFO investigator David Rudiak, who had a particular interest in deciphering the memo, and whose research into its contents continues to this day. Rudiak says of his work in this particular arena:

> "There is no question that Ramey's message, even when greatly enlarged and then enhanced by computer, is a very difficult read...However, there are various keywords and phrases that can be readily seen by anyone, even in lower resolution scans of the message first analyzed in 1999 by a number of people. These keywords and phrases unambiguously prove that there is no truth whatsoever to the various Air Force 'explanations,' be they the original 1947 'weather balloon' story, or the Air Forces updated 'Mogul balloon' and 'crash dummies.'"

There is very little doubt that the memo includes the words "in the 'disc' they will ship." Far more controversially, Rudiak concludes from his analysis that the words "operation at the ranch" and "the victims of the wreck" can also be seen.

* * * * * * * * * * *

"IT MIGHT PROVIDE A CLUE ABOUT WHAT FELL NEAR ROSWELL"

Of the memo itself, Kevin Randle said in 2015:

> "The best case of provenance that I have ever seen is the Ramey Memo. We have a picture of Ramey holding

> the document, we have been able to interview the photographer, and we know the date on which it was taken because we have not only a dated document that was transmitted with the picture, but it appeared in newspapers around the country the next day. The only point of dispute is what the memo actually says. Parts of it are easily read and others are obscured to the point where it is sometimes just a best guess. If the memo could be completely deciphered it might provide a clue about what fell near Roswell and would be some of the best documentation available."

Randle also noted in 2015: "While 'Victims of the wreck' might not take us immediately to the extraterrestrial, it would certainly start us on the path."

Then, in 2016, there was this from Kevin: "Several have suggested that the word is not 'victims' but is 'viewing.' It does contain the right number of letters and it does begin with a "V," but it also alters the importance of the Ramey Memo if that is correct."

The matter was still not over. *Open Minds* said on June 22, 2016: "Last week UFO researcher and author Kevin Randle posted news of a $10,000 reward for anyone who can decipher the text of a memo seen in a picture of what is supposedly debris from the Roswell UFO crash site. Some UFO researchers doubt the debris in the photo is actually from the object that crashed outside Roswell in July, 1947, and believe the text in the memo proves it. Many find those claims to be hard to accept. Especially after looking at a magnified version of the memo. It seems that something should be able to be deciphered. While not all researchers agree with Rudiak's interpretation, many UFO researchers do believe there is something there. Apparently, an anonymous donor also feels strongly that there is something important to be discovered in the memo."

* * * * * * * * * * * *

DEFINING A "VICTIM"

There is no doubt that the Ramey Memo is extremely thought-provoking, in terms of what it might say, and in relation to the events which occurred in 1947-era New Mexico. A careful study of the text does suggest that the word "victims" could actually be the correct one. As Kevin Randle notes, however, "viewing" is an equally good candidate, too. The latter makes sense, considering the fact that the debris was on show for J. Bond Johnson to photograph. And for Johnson to *view.* Kevin is also right on target when he states that if the real word *is* "viewing," then it most definitely lessens the importance that is generated by the word "victims." After all, if there were victims, then the object which came down was clearly neither a weather-balloon nor a Mogul balloon. And no-one of a sane mind would ever describe a crash-test dummy as a victim.

There is, however, an issue that seldom gets discussed when it comes to the matter of the Ramey Memo. The full-on "Roswell was E.T." believer would most likely say that a reference to "victims" is the smoking-gun we have sought for so long; a smoking-gun which makes a reference to the aliens found on-board the wrecked UFO, or somewhere else on the huge Foster Ranch. But, does it, really? Well, it certainly *could*; but I suggest not. And I will tell you exactly why.

I find the use of that *specific* word – "victims" – to be both odd and potentially revealing. I would have thought that terms like "the crew," "the pilots," "the spacemen," or "the beings" would have been far more appropriate when it came to describing strange-looking entities that arrived from another world with no warning. "Victims" suggests something else. In fact, I would go so far to say that just the word "victims" itself has an undeniable human, even emotion-filled, quality attached to it, rather than something we might apply to a definitively unearthly alien.

Let's take a look at the definitions for "victim" that Merriam-Webster provides. They include:

- "one that is acted on and usually adversely affected by a force or agent"
- "one that is injured, destroyed, or sacrificed under any of various conditions"
- "one that is subjected to oppression, hardship, or mistreatment"
- "one that is tricked or duped"

If the "human experiment" angle for Roswell is the correct one – as I believe it to be – then the terminology used by Merriam-Webster to define a "victim" is most apt. After all, there is no doubt that those used in the 1940s-era experiments were "adversely affected by a force or agent." Few would deny they were "injured, destroyed, or sacrificed." And they were certainly "subjected to oppression, hardship, or mistreatment."

Finally, but still on the matter of that controversial sentence in the Ramey Memo, there is the issue of the word "wreck." It seems very strange that such a word would have been used to describe what the military was assuring the media was just a flimsy weather-balloon. It's equally odd terminology to use for a Mogul balloon – the theory the Air Force came up with in 1994. "Wreck" implies something pretty physically substantial that has been significantly damaged, rather than the torn and scattered remains of a balloon whether large or small.

So, while the Ramey Memo is not the ultimate smoking-gun that proves *any* particular theory, there's no doubt that it keeps the Roswell flame burning, whatever the answer.

CONCLUSIONS

NOW it's time for us to make a few final observations. For the last few decades, Roswell has been UFOlogy's number-one case. It's a field of research that is always looking for proof that UFOs exist. And, by proof, I mean hard solid evidence that can be examined and studied – if, of course, "they" would only "tell us the truth." As I write this, seventy years have gone by since Kenneth Arnold kicked off the flying saucer controversy – after encountering a squadron of unidentified aerial vehicles near Mt. Rainier, Washington State. And, although we have masses of material, eye-witness testimony, photos, declassified files, etc., the fact is that we still don't have hard evidence of – or definitive answers for – what UFOs actually are. Roswell, however, UFO researchers say, theoretically offers us those answers. If only, that is, we could uncover the bodies, the wreckage, the old files, and so on. And presuming, of course, that Roswell was an alien event and not something else. Such as something down-to-earth and which still has to remain hidden at all costs.

The fact is that UFOlogy is not just seeking hard, undeniable proof that UFOs exist. Much of UFOlogy is *desperate* to find pro-E.T. evidence for Roswell, chiefly so that all those decades of research won't be seen as a waste of time. Those UFO researchers now in their sixties, seventies and eighties are faced with meeting the Grim Reaper before they get to see the doors to the "secret Roswell hangar" opened wide. For those researchers, the answers *have* to come, before it's all too late. And they have to come *soon*. Roswell is to them what Moby Dick was to Captain Ahab.

So, for those who conclude that aliens crashed back in July 1947, the Roswell affair – with its large number of first-, second-, and third-hand witnesses, and with the government having changed its stance on what happened more than a couple of times – is the one that could really tip the scales. And, with the scales tipped, the world would know that the UFO community was right all along and it was all worth it. All thanks to Roswell.

There's very little doubt in my mind that when UFOlogists see the word "Roswell" prominently referenced in a new online article, there's an immediate sense of "Maybe, this time, we really have it nailed." I saw just such a thing happen when the fiasco known as "the Roswell Slides" surfaced a few years back. For those who don't know the pathetic saga, it revolves around a photograph of a mummified child which was, for a while, touted as one of the bodies from the Roswell crash. The whole thing was an embarrassment, one that is best forgotten.

There's another reason why Roswell is so important, but from a very different perspective. It gets to the crux of this book. If, one day, Roswell is conclusively proven *not* to have been an extraterrestrial event – maybe, instead, some dark and murky domestic experiment of the kinds detailed in this book – then I firmly believe that the UFO community will have a collective breakdown / meltdown of epic proportions and from which it will never recover. Shaking knees, breathing slowly into paper bags, stomach ulcers, antidepressants, and uncontrollable bladders will be commonplace. Don't even get me started on out-of-control bowel movements.

In that sense, UFOlogy is desperate to see Roswell confirmed as an extraterrestrial event. UFOlogy can barely consider Roswell as anything else. For so many, such a situation is utterly unthinkable.

So, again, whenever Roswell pops up – and particularly so amid rumors that "something big" is coming – there is a dire and pressing need, and a desperate yearning, for something tangible. So, everyone clicks on the link, praying for the definitive breakthrough that has consistently failed to surface; the breakthrough that only "St. Roswell" can (maybe) deliver into UFOlogy's eager hands.

Roswell has been elevated and championed as an E.T. event to such an incredible degree that it can – single-handedly – completely make or break UFOlogy. *Forever.* However you look at the case – and whatever your personal opinion on what happened in '47 on the Foster Ranch – that's why the incident remains so incredibly important.

My personal view is that for UFOlogy it will be break and not make. Here's why…

Despite the words of the naysayers, and those who hope and pray I am wrong, the fact is there exists a large body of material that strongly supports the "secret experiment" theory. Such was the controversial and incriminating nature of the files and the experiments, they were buried decades ago – and they remain buried. Or maybe, as I have suggested, all of that same incriminating data has been relegated to the furnace and the shredder. But, that doesn't prevent a case from being made.

Although pro-UFO researchers and investigators make a big fuss about the discoveries on the Foster Ranch, they seldom highlight the fact that, prior to the events of early July 1947, rancher Mack Brazel found the remains of *two* weather-balloons on the property. That is an important thing to note, as is this: there is no doubt that much of the material scooped up by Brazel was very balloon-like. And, we know that balloons had fallen on the ranch previously. *Military* balloons. *Twice.* If that doesn't strike you as being notable, well, it sure as shit should. Also, recall the words of Sue Farnsworth. She said: "We were used to finding 'funny things' from White Sands on our ranch all the time, but this was clearly something different judging by the military reaction."

White Sands, New Mexico (Nick Redfern)

In light of all this, few can deny that military devices – of varying degrees of secrecy – were dropping from the skies over New Mexico, in the late 1940s. Let's see what else is on the table.

Also in 1947, we have the following, found in FBI files declassified under the terms of the Freedom of Information Act: "Special Agent S. W. Reynolds of the Liaison Section, while discussing the above captioned phenomena with Lieutenant Colonel Garrett of the Air Forces Intelligence, expressed the possibility that *flying discs were, in fact, a very highly classified experiment of the Army or Navy* [italics mine]. Mr. Reynolds was very much surprised when Colonel Garrett not only agreed that this was a possibility, but confidentially stated it was his personal opinion that such was a probability. Colonel Garrett indicated that a Mr. [name deleted], who is a scientist attached to the Air Forces Intelligence, was of the same opinion."

Moving onto 1949, there is the highly intriguing theory of the staff at Fort Detrick (at the time, Camp Detrick) that, in the final year of the Second World War, 1945, a Japanese Fugo balloon came down *in* Lincoln County and unleashed a deadly cargo of plague-infected insects – such as fleas – and which eventually took hold, leading to the unfortunate death of the young boy at Fort Stanton, four years later. Fort Stanton being a place that plays a major role in this whole story and which, at various times, held Japanese "enemy aliens" and handicapped people. It's a facility located hardly any distance at all from where Brazel made his discovery.

Onto the early 1950s, we have the shocking Sunshine program and its outrageous activities relative to body-snatching and highly controversial human experimentation. As for the 1960s, 1969, we have the testimony of the family of Melvin Brown, who, while stationed at the Roswell Army Air Field in 1947, briefly saw the Roswell bodies and told his wife and children that they could have "passed for Chinese" and looked Asian. Alien "Grays" they were not.

From the 1970s, there are the recollections of John A. Price. In a nearby town, Hagerman, he encountered a group of unusual children: all roughly four- to four-and-a-half-feet in height, with large and hairless heads and tiny noses and ears. In the following decade, one of Price's sources told him of people with strange appearances held at Fort Stanton: "There were some pretty deformed young men there, several of which could be of alien nature. We only went by what we were told; please don't tell anyone. Mongoloid large heads, small ears, pin heads who could function and had shrill voices. They were supposed to be of incest, but from their looks – Outa-space."

There was also an engineer, Robert Betz. Price said of Betz's views on the Foster Ranch incident that: "Robert was convinced that the Roswell crash could be explained away as a top secret project of flying saucer design and that the bodies were midgets."

Now, let's move into the 1990s, when things really started to heat up. In 1991, Leonard Stringfield published an account of strange bodies secretly flown to Los Alamos from late 1945 to 1947. From where? The rumor was Japan. They were small corpses, with oversized heads and large eyes. Their skin was severely burned – as if they had been in some kind of accident. Nurse Marian Ehart grudgingly confirmed that she knew something of this story – but preferred not to say too much about it, beyond confirming the basic data.

In this same time frame, and through 1993, John Keel was pursuing the Japanese connection to Roswell. Keel said: "If such a project was launched, they would have selected the smallest, lightest volunteers available...It is also likely they might have expired during the trip...their complexions would have been very odd, discolored by the cold...If even one such volunteer balloonist attempted the trip and crashed, we would have the answer to all those rumors and legends which persist to this day."

In 1997, which was Roswell's 50th anniversary, two interesting, and relevant, developments surfaced. One was the publication of Philip Corso's book, *The Day after Roswell*, a book filled with controversy. Particularly notable is the fact that Corso was good friends with Major General Charles Willoughby, a central character in the secret program to get Japan's Unit 731 files into the hands of the United States' military. Also in 1997, *Popular Mechanics* magazine revealed that its staff had been tipped off to a forthcoming release of documents that would reveal the Japanese link to Roswell. As it happens, such files did not surface. That the magazine was given the story, however, suggests that behind the scenes someone in government wanted the story put into the public domain - even though they were thwarted from doing so. Or maybe, they backed off due to fear and possible consequences of the deadly type. Both scenarios are equally plausible.

Between 2001 and 2004, I interviewed the people who provided the material that appeared in my *Body Snatchers in the Desert* book. Also in 2004, the original printed manuscript of my book vanished from the offices of Simon & Schuster in New York – something which provoked a great deal of debate and concern. Months after the book was published, in the summer of 2005, Australian UFO authority, Keith Basterfield, revealed he had secured testimony from an Australian source who told him a near-identical story. Handicapped people, gigantic balloons, and secret projects – all of the key ingredients were there.

The year 2005 was also revealing for two other reasons: (a) the "coincidence" of my book being published on June 21, 2005, and the fact that this was the very same day the Nazi War Criminal Records Interagency Working Group began addressing further wartime Japanese war crimes, including those of Unit 731, and (b) that twenty-four hours later, I was contacted by a representative of the IWG and who expressed interest in *Body Snatchers in the Desert.*

Then, in 2007, there were the revelations concerning acclaimed cinema legend Billy Wilder, Roswell, psychological warfare operations, and the 1970 movie, *The Private Life of Sherlock*

Holmes – all of which suggested that, while working with psy-op staff, Wilder learned at least something about Roswell. Maybe more than we will ever know.

Kathy Kasten's voluminous files, which I received in 2012 and that I carefully studied in 2013 and 2014, added much more to the issue of the role that Fort Stanton played in the Roswell event, and introduced us to the secret role of William Randolph Lovelace II. Both 2015 and 2016 revealed more on the "victims of the wreck" controversy, as it relates to what has become known as the "Ramey Memo." And, you have seen my argument on the "victims" angle. Aliens? Nope. And, that pretty much brings us up to date.

If one puts all of these threads, sources, leads, and data together – which span from 1947 to 2016 - what one gets is a picture that is far from pretty. The picture is actually just about as bleak and terrible as it could possibly be.

As this book now comes to a close, I will leave you with one final thing to ponder on. There is one very important issue that few people ever think about when it comes to the Foster Ranch crash. It does, however, get right to the very heart of the incident and what did or did not happen. If the debris, and possibly bodies and craft, recovered outside of Roswell, New Mexico in the summer of 1947 had extra-terrestrial origins, then why did the aliens' comrades fail to attempt to recover the priceless materials before elements of the U.S. military appeared on the scene?

After all, even a cursory study of UFO history reveals that aliens are supposedly able to walk through walls, abduct people against their will and then return them to their homes without being caught in the act, steal and / or mutilate cattle right under the noses of outraged farmers, and traverse the universe. They are even said to have snatched military and private aircraft in flight – planes that were never seen again. Neither were their crews. So in light of all their incredible skills, why weren't the assumed aliens able to scoop up a few bodies and a bunch of scattered debris from an isolated ranch in New Mexico? It's hardly as if everything took place in Times Square with thousands of amazed onlookers crowding around.

This question is echoed by film-maker Paul Kimball: "... surely they would have moved to recover any crashed excursion module as quickly as possible, a process which, considering the advanced technology that the aliens must possess in order to get 'here' from 'there' is something that they would have accomplished before Mack Brazel discovered the debris field and then alerted the military, even if that involved simply disintegrating the debris field so as to leave no trace behind of the crash."

If E.T.s did crash, then a number of possibilities spring to mind:

- The aliens wanted to introduce themselves to us in the form of a staged-crash, and as vulnerable, mortal beings, to whom we could possibly relate, and without being confronted by infinitely advanced intelligences that might blow our minds.
- The event was the result of a "Trojan Horse"-style scenario - also staged by the other-worldly ones, but for far more sinister purposes, such as perhaps attempting to expose us to deadly alien viruses, but in a seemingly innocent and accidental fashion.

Roswell today (Nick Redfern)

- The aliens, far away from home, may not actually have been too far in advance of us - perhaps a century or so - and simply didn't have the adequate resources and reserves at-hand to engage in a hasty retrieval. Possible, though the evidence suggests the true UFO phenomenon is millennia in front of us – probably more.

There is, of course, another theory. It's a far more probable one. Aliens didn't try and recover the Roswell wreckage because...*what happened at Roswell didn't involve aliens...*

BIBLIOGRAPHY

Albarelli, Hank P, Jr. "*CIA Denial of Coddling Nazis Far From the Truth.*" http://www.voltairenet.org/article168573.html. February 26, 2011.

Arakawa, H. *Basic Principles of the Balloon Bomb.* Tokyo, Japan: Meteorological Research Institute.

Basterfield, Keith. "*Jacobsen, Redfern and an Adelaide informant.*" http://ufos-scientificresearch.blogspot.com/2011/07/jacobsen-redfern-and-adelaide-informant.html. July 8, 2011.

Berlitz, Charles & Moore, William. *The Roswell Incident.* London, U.K.: Granada Publishing, Ltd., 1980.

"*Billy Wilder Biography.*" http://www.biography.com/people/billy-wilder-9531169. 2016.

Bishop, Greg. *Project Beta.* NY: Simon & Schuster, 2005.

Bower, Tom. *The Paperclip Conspiracy.* Boston, MA: Little, Brown, 1987.

Bragalia, Anthony. "*Anthony Bragalia's reply to our Truman Syndrome post.*" http://ufocon.blogspot.com/2008/08/anthony-bragalias-reply-to-our-truman.html. August 15, 2008.

Bragalia, Anthony. "*Area 51 Book Exposed: Jacobsen's Secret Source Revealed with Interview.*" http://www.theufochronicles.com/2011/05/area-51-book-exposed-secret-source.html. May 31, 2011.

Bragalia, Anthony. "*Was There a Chaplain at the Roswell Crash?*" http://www.ufodigest.com/news/1009/chaplain.php. October 14, 2009.

Burgess, Colin. *Sigma 7: The Six Mercury Orbits of Walter M. Schirra, Jr.* NY: Springer, 2016.

Cannon, Martin. "*Roswell: Truth and Consequences.*" https://archive.org/stream/pdf_martincannon_roswelltruthandconsequences/Martin%20Cannon%20-%20Roswell%20Truth%20and%20Consequences_djvu.txt. 2017.

Carey, Thomas J. & Schmitt, Donald R. *The Children of Roswell.* Wayne, NJ: New Page Books, 2016.

Carey, Thomas J. & Schmitt, Donald, R. *Witness to Roswell.* Wayne, NJ: New Page Books, 2009.

Clarke, David. *How UFOs Conquered the World.* London, U.K.: Aurum Press, Ltd., 2015.

Clarke, David. "*The Scottish Roswell.*" https://drdavidclarke.co.uk/2015/05/03/the-scottish-roswell-2/. May 3, 2015.

Corso, Philip J & Birnes, J. William. *The Day After Roswell.* NY: Simon & Schuster, 1997.

"*Death Mills American Government Film.*" https://www.youtube.com/watch?v=sv4MXdFKfi4. 2016.

Department of Energy. *Advisory Committee on Human Radiation Experiments: Final Report.* Washington, D.C.: U.S. Government Printing Office, 1995.

Desbough, Brian. *They Cast No Shadows.* Bloomington, IN: iUniverse, 2002.

Edwards, Frank. *Flying Saucers – Serious Business.* NY: Lyle Stuart, 1966.

"*Enemy Alien.*" https://en.wikipedia.org/wiki/Enemy_alien. 2017.

Farrell, Joseph P. "*Roswell and the Reich.*" Kempton, IL: Adventures Unlimited Press, 2010.

Federal Bureau of Investigation. "*Bacteriological Warfare in the United States.*" Declassified 2006.

Federal Bureau of Investigation. "*UFO.*" https://vault.fbi.gov/UFO. 2016.

"*Fort Stanton, NM.*" http://fortstanton.org/. 2017.

Friedman, Stanton T. & Berliner, Don. *Crash at Corona.* NY: Paragon House, 1992.

Friedman, Stanton T. & Moore, William, L. "*The Roswell Incident: Beginning of the Cosmic Watergate.*" Proceedings, MUFON Symposium, Cambridge, MA, 1981.

Friedman, Stanton T. "*Nick Redfern's Body Snatchers in the Desert: The Horrible Truth at the Heart of the Roswell Story.*" http://www.stantonfriedman.com/index.php?ptp=book_reviews&fdt=2005.06.15. June 15, 2005.

Galde, Phyllis (editor). *The Best of Roswell.* Lakeville, MN: Galde Press, Inc., 2007.

General Accounting Office. *Results of a Search for Records Concerning the 1947 Crash Near Roswell, New Mexico.* Washington, D.C.: U.S. Government Printing Office, July 28, 1995.

Goebel, Greg. "*Cold War Balloon Flights 1945:1965.*" http://www.airvectors.net/avbloon_3.html. 2017.

Good, Timothy. *Alien Contact*. NY: William Morrow, 1992.

"*Grave Site of Marian Jo Ehart*." https://billiongraves.com/grave/Marian-Jo-Ehart/5756968#/ August 11, 2013.

Guest, E.A. "*The Other Paradigm*." Fate, April 2005.

"*History of Fort Stanton, The*." http://fortstanton.org/history/. 2017.

"*Interagency Working Group: Meeting Minutes: 06/21/05*." https://www.archives.gov/iwg/meetings/minutes/minutes-062105.html. June 21, 2005.

Jacobsen, Annie. *Area 51: An Uncensored History of America's Top Secret Military Base*. NY: Back Bay Books, 2012.

Kathy Kasten's files, donated to the author in 2012.

Keel, John. "*Return of the Fugos*." *Fate*, April 1993.

Keel, John. '*The Fugo Balloons*." *Fate*, March 1990.

Keith, Jim. "*Roswell UFO Bombshell*." *Fate*, January 2000.

Koren, Yehuda & Negev, Eilat. *Giants: The Dwarfs of Auschwitz*. NY: MJF Books, 2013.

"*Lovelace's Woman in Space Program*." https://history.nasa.gov/flats.html. 2017.

"*Mantell Case – 1948*." http://www.mufon.com/mantell-case---1948.html. 2017.

Marcel, Jesse & Marcel, Linda. *The Roswell Legacy*. Wayne, NJ: New Page Books, 2009.

"*Marian J. Ehart*." https://www.coloradolicensing.org/marian-j-ehart. 2017.

Mikesh, Robert C. *Japan's World War II Balloon Bomb Attacks on North America.* Washington, D.C.: Smithsonian Institution Press, 1997.

Moore, William, L. *"Crashed Saucers: Evidence in the Search for Proof."* Proceedings, MUFON Symposium, St. Louis, MO, 1985.

Moore, William L. *The Roswell Investigation.* Burbank, CA: William L. Moore Publications and Research, 1982.

National Security Agency UFO files. Declassified under the terms of the Freedom of Information Act.

Newman, Bernard. *The Flying Saucer.* Yardley, PA: Westholme Publishing, LLC, 2010.

Patton, Anthony. "*Man in the Moon.*" https://hms.harvard.edu/news/harvard-medicine/man-moon. 2017.

Pflock, Karl T. *Roswell in Perspective.* Mt. Rainier, MD: The Fund for UFO Research, 1994.

Pflock, Karl T. "*What's Really Behind the Flying Saucers? A New Twist on Aztec.*" San Antonio, TX: The Anomalist, 2000.

Price, John A. *Roswell – A Quest for the Truth.* San Diego, CA: Truth Seeker, Co., Inc., 1997.

"*Private Life of Sherlock Holmes, The.*" http://www.imdb.com/title/tt0066249/. 2017.

Quimby, Edith H. & McCune, Donovan. "*Uptake of Radioactive Iodine by the Normal and Disordered Thyroid Gland in Children.*" *Biology Division Bulletin* of the Clinton National Laboratory, November 3, 1947.

Ramsey, Scott, Ramsey, Suzanne & Thayer, Frank. *The Aztec UFO Incident.* Wayne, NJ: New Page Books, 2016.

Randle. Kevin D. "*Annie Jacobsen, Area 51 and UFOs.*" http://kevinrandle.blogspot.com/2011/05/annie-jacobsen-area-51-and-ufos.html. May 23, 2011.

Randle, Kevin D. *Crash.* Wayne, NJ: New Page Books, 2010.

Randle, Kevin. "*Ramey Memo Update.*" http://kevinrandle.blogspot.com/2015/09/ramey-memo-update.html. September 26, 2015.

Randle, Kevin D. "*Roswell Explained – Again.*" *Fate*, September 2005.

Randle, Kevin D. *The Roswell Encyclopedia.* NY: Harper-Collins, 2000.

Randle, Kevin D. "*Viewing vs Victims of the Wreck.*" http://kevinrandle.blogspot.com/2016/04/viewing-vs-victims-of-wreck.html. April 30, 2016.

Randle, Kevin D. & Schmitt, Donald R. *The Truth About the UFO Crash at Roswell.* NY: M. Evans, 1994.

Randle, Kevin D. & Schmitt, Donald R. *UFO Crash at Roswell.* NY: Avon Books, 1991.

Redfern, Nick. "*A Response from Nick Redfern.*" *Fate*, September 2005.

Redfern, Nick. "*Body Snatchers: Before and Beyond.*" *Darklore Volume III*, edited by Greg Taylor. Brisbane, Australia: Daily Grail Publishing, 2009.

Redfern, Nick. *Body Snatchers in the Desert.* NY: Simon & Schuster, 2005.

Redfern, Nick. *Close Encounters of the Fatal Kind.* Wayne, NJ: New Page Books, 2014.

Redfern, Nick. *Final Events*. San Antonio, TX: Anomalist Books, 2010.

Redfern, Nick. *Men in Black*. Bracey, VA: Lisa Hagan Books, 2015.

Redfern, Nick. *On the Trail of the Saucer Spies*. San Antonio, TX: Anomalist Books, 2006.

Redfern, Nick. *The FBI Files*. London, U.K.: Simon & Schuster, 1998.

Redfern, Nick. *The NASA Conspiracies*. Wayne, NJ: New Page Books, 2010.

Rojas, Alejandro. "*$10,000 reward offered to decipher Roswell UFO memo*." http://www.openminds.tv/10000-reward-offered-to-decipher-roswell-ufo-memo/37759. June 22, 2016.

Rudiak, David. "*Roswell Proof*." http://www.roswellproof.com/. 2001.

Rudiak, David. "*Roswell Smoking Gun, the Ramey Memo*." http://www.ufocasebook.com/rameymemo.html. 2001.

Schwarz, Brian. "*The Ghosts of Unit 731*." http://www.americanthinker.com/blog/2005/09/the_ghosts_of_unit_731.html. September 17, 2005.

Scully, Frank. *Behind the Flying Saucers*. NY: Henry Holt & Co., 1950.

Smith, Paul H. "*What is Remote Viewing?*" http://www.irva.org/remote-viewing/definition.html. 2017.

"*SOX2 Anophthalmia Syndrome*." https://ghr.nlm.nih.gov/condition/sox2-anophthalmia-syndrome. 2017.

Stringfield, Leonard. *UFO Crash / Retrievals: The Inner Sanctum.* Cincinnati, OH: published privately, 1991.

Taylor, Greg. "*New Roswell Revelations.*" http://dailygrail.com/news/new-roswell-revelations. May 1, 2009.

Tonnies, Mac. "*Paul Kimball weighs in on the Roswell Incident.*" http://posthumanblues.blogspot.com/2008/06/paul-kimball-weighs-in-on-roswell.html. June 22, 2008.

Tonnies, Mac. *The Cryptoterrestrials.* San Antonio, TX: Anomalist Books, 2010.

Tonnies, Mac. "*The Roswell Controversy.*" http://posthumanblues.blogspot.com/2009/02/roswell-controversy.html. February 18, 2009.

UFO. Vol. 9, No. 2, 1994.

United States Air Force. "*Holloman Air Force Base Range Safety, 1947-1959.*" July 14, 1960.

United States Air Force press conference. The Pentagon, Washington, D.C., July 4, 1997.

United States Air Force. *The Roswell Report: Case Closed.* Washington, D.C.: U.S. Government Printing Office, 1997.

United States Air Force. *The Roswell Report: Fact vs. Fiction in the New Mexico Desert.* Washington, D.C.: U.S. Government Printing Office, 1995.

University of New Mexico. "*New Mexican Had Lookout for 'Japanese Germs.'*" Press release, 1945.

University of New Mexico. "*No Jap Balloon, Light in the Sky was a Meteorite.*" Press Release, 1945.

"*Victim*." https://www.merriam-webster.com/dictionary/victim. 2017.

Webber, Bert. *Silent Siege III: Japanese Attacks on North America in World War II*. Medford, OR: Webb Research Group Publishers, 1997.

Weeks, Linton. "*Beware of Japanese Balloon Bombs*." http://www.npr.org/sections/npr-history-dept/2015/01/20/375820191/beware-of-japanese- balloon-bombs. January 20, 2015.

"*William Randolph Lovelace II*." https://en.wikipedia.org/wiki/William_Randolph_Lovelace_II. 2017.

Williams, Peter & Wallace, David. *Unit 31: Japan's Secret Biological Warfare in World War II*. NY: The Free Press, 1989.

Wilson, Jim. "Roswell Plus 50." *Popular Mechanics*, July 1997.

Wood, Robert M. & Redfern, Nick. *Alien Viruses*. Rochester, NY: Richard Dolan Press, 2013.

Wood, Ryan S. *Majic Eyes Only*. Broomfield, CO: Wood Enterprises, 2005.

"*World War II Enemy Alien Control Program Overview*." https://www.archives.gov/research/immigration/enemy-aliens-overview.html. 2017.

Wu, Tien-Wei. "*A Preliminary Review of Studies of Japanese Biological Warfare and Unit 731 in the United States*." http://www.zzwave.com/cmfweb/wiihist/germwar/731rev.htm. 2017.

Zagami, Leo Lyon. *Confessions of an Illuminati*. San Francisco, CA: CCC Publishing, 2016.

ACKNOWLEDGMENTS

I would like to offer my sincere thanks to my agent, friend and publisher, Lisa Hagan; my editor and co-publisher, Beth Wareham; book-designer, Simon Hartshorne; and UFO researcher, Keith Basterfield.

ABOUT THE AUTHOR

NICK Redfern is the author of 40 books on UFOs, lake-monsters, zombies, and Hollywood scandal, including *Women in Black*; *Men in Black*; and *365 Days of UFOs.* Nick has appeared on many TV shows, including the BBC's Out of This World; the SyFy Channel's Proof Positive; the History Channel's Monster Quest, America's Book of Secrets, Ancient Aliens and *UFO Hunters*; the National Geographic Channel's Paranatural; and MSNBC's Countdown with Keith Olbermann.

He can be contacted at his blog: http://nickredfernfortean.blogspot.com

16155425R00140

Printed in Great Britain
by Amazon